Practical Geometry for Art Students

Here, for example, are four problems (see page 20) constructed on the same principle, which being once grasped, will
help the student to solve every problem in which that principle
is involved :—

PRINCIPLE—" *The angle in a semicircle is a right angle.*"

PROBLEM—1. To draw a line perpendicular to a given line from
a given point.

2. To construct a right-angled triangle, given its
hypotenuse and one side.

3. To construct a square on a given line.

4. To construct an oblong, given the diagonal and
one side.

Though this book contains over 200 problems and exercises,
it might have been considerably enlarged, for applications of
these principles can be multiplied almost *ad infinitum.*

It has not been deemed necessary to do this, for, indepen-
dently of adding to the cost, it would have interfered with the
plan of the work, which has been designed to encourage the
student to exercise thought in his study, and to enable him to
solve any problem or exercise in Practical Geometry whose construction is based on the principles here illustrated.

J. C.

ST. JOHN'S WOOD,
Oct. 1880.

CONTENTS.

——◆◆——

INTRODUCTION.

GEOMETRY (*Ge*, the earth, and *metron*, a measure) originally signified the art of measuring the earth or any distances on it. It now denotes the science of magnitudes in general, and treats of their various properties and relations, its principles being founded upon a few axioms or self-evident truths.

Practical Geometry is the application of these principles to the measurement and drawing of lines, and the construction of figures. It is a subject of the greatest importance to all who are engaged in mechanical pursuits, and a knowledge of it is essential to the Architect, the Designer, the Engineer, and the Surveyor. It is, moreover, an important educational agent, furnishing, as it does, a training in habits of accuracy and neatness, and culti-vating true ideas of form and proportion. That this study may be of benefit to the student, it will be necessary for him to exercise the greatest care in his work, for slovenliness will certainly expose itself and lead to disappointment and failure. His instruments, which need not at first be many or costly, must be kept in good condition.

The following are necessary :—

   1. A pair of compasses, with moveable pen and pencil joint.
   2. A pair of dividers.
   3. Black-lead pencils H and HB or F.
   4. A drawing pen for lines.
   5. A set of scales on a six-inch rule, and protractor.
   6. Two set-squares or angles.

In addition, these will be found useful :—

   7. A drawing-board and three or four drawing-pins.
   8. A T-square.

TERMS USED IN PRACTICAL GEOMETRY.

A point is that which has position but not magnitude.
In practice it is represented by a dot, or thus ⊙ ; but as the smallest dot we can make has magnitude, the centre of that dot is the point we wish to indicate.

LINES.

A line has length without breadth.

A straight line is the shortest distance between two points.
In practice we adopt various modes of representing lines, as— strong, fine, dotted, and chain lines. Fig. 1.

A curve is a line which is nowhere straight. Fig. 2.

Parallels are lines which are the same distance apart from end to end, however long they may be made. Fig. 3.

ANGLES.

An angle is the inclination of two straight lines which meet in a point called the vertex of the angle.
The magnitude of an angle does not depend on the length of the lines which form it, but upon their inclination to one another.

A right angle. When one straight line standing on another makes the adjacent angles equal, each of the angles is called a *right angle.* Fig. 4. The line A B is said to be perpendicular to the other C D, which is a horizontal line.

An acute angle is less than a right angle. Fig. 5.

An obtuse angle is greater than a right angle. Fig. 6. The lines E F (Fig. 5) and K L (Fig. 6) are termed *oblique or slant lines.*

TRIANGLES.

A triangle is a figure bounded by three straight lines, and having, therefore, three angles.

An equilateral triangle has its three sides equal. Fig. 7.

An isosceles triangle has two of its sides equal. Fig. 8.

A scalene triangle has all its sides unequal. Fig. 9.

A right-angled triangle is one which has a right angle, the side opposite being termed the *hypotenuse.* Fig. 10.

An obtuse-angled triangle is one which has an obtuse angle. Fig. 11.

An acute-angled triangle is one which has all its angles acute. Fig. 12.

Note.—An equilateral triangle is always acute angled. An isosceles triangle may be right angled, acute, or obtuse. A scalene triangle may also be right angled, acute, or obtuse. The *altitude* of a triangle is the straight line drawn from its vertex perpendicularly to its base, as A B, Fig. 12.

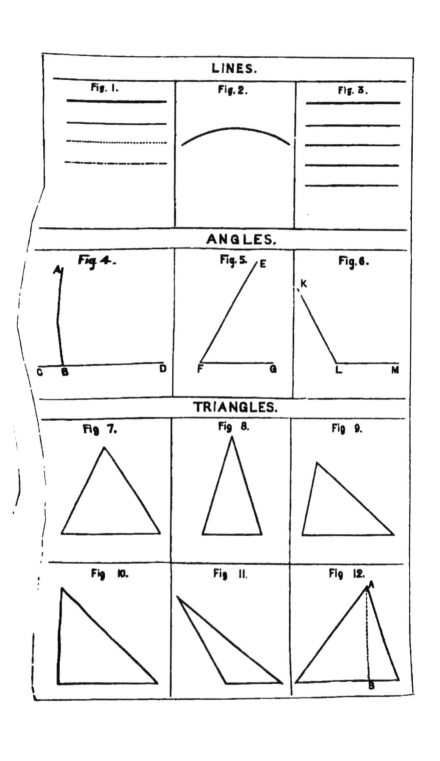

LINES.

Fig. 1.   Fig. 2.   Fig. 3.

ANGLES.

Fig. 4.   Fig. 5.   Fig. 6.

TRIANGLES.

Fig 7.   Fig 8.   Fig 9.

Fig 10.   Fig 11.   Fig 12.

TERMS (Continued).

QUADRILATERALS.

Quadrilateral figures are bounded by four sides. If the opposite sides of a quadrilateral are parallel to each other it is termed a *parallelogram*.

Of Parallelograms:

A *Square* has all its sides equal and all its angles right angles. Fig. 13.

A *Rectangle* or *Oblong* has all its angles right angles, but its adjacent sides are unequal. · Fig. 14.

A *Rhombus* has its sides equal, but its adjacent angles unequal. Fig. 15.

A *Rhomboid* has its adjacent sides unequal and its adjacent angles unequal. Fig. 16.

When only two sides of a quadrilateral are parallel it is termed a *Trapezoid.* Fig. 17. When none of its sides are parallel it is termed a *Trapezium*. A Trapezium, one of whose diagonals divides it into two unequal isosceles triangles, is called by some geometers a *Trapezion*, by others a *Kite*. Fig. 18.

POLYGONS.

A *Polygon* is a rectilineal figure bounded by more than four straight lines. If it is equilateral and equiangular it is termed a *Regular Polygon*. A *Pentagon* has five sides, Fig. 19; a *Hexagon* six, Fig. 20; a *Heptagon* seven, Fig. 21; an *Octagon* eight; a *Nonagon* nine; a *Decagon* ten; an *Undecagon* eleven; a *Dodecagon* twelve.

THE CIRCLE AND ITS PARTS.

A *Circle* is a plane figure bounded by one curve called the *Circumference*, every part of which is equally distant from a point within, called the *Centre*. Fig. 22.

The Radius is a straight line drawn from the centre to the circumference, as A B.

The Diameter of a circle is a straight line drawn through the centre and terminating both ways in the circumference, as C D.

A *Chord* is a straight line joining any two points in the circumference.

An *Arc* is any part of the circumference.

A *Segment* is any part of a circle bounded by an arc and its chord. Fig. 23.

A *Semicircle* is half a circle, or a segment cut off by a diameter.

A *Sector* is any part of a circle bounded by an arc and two radii. Fig. 24.

A *Quadrant* is a sector which is a fourth part of a circle.

A *Sextant* is a sector which is the sixth part of a circle.

Concentric Circles are those which have the same centre. Fig. 25.

A *Tangent* is a straight line which *touches* a circle or curve in one point, and which being produced does not *cut* it, as E F.

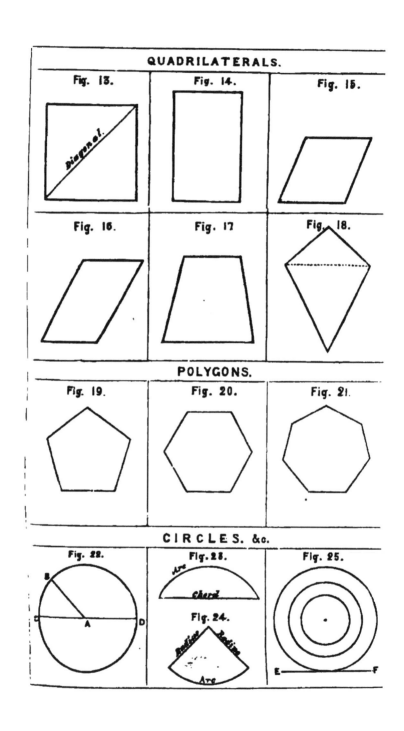

QUADRILATERALS.

Fig. 13.

Fig. 14.

Fig. 15.

Diagonal.

Fig. 16.

Fig. 17

Fig. 18.

POLYGONS.

Fig. 19.

Fig. 20.

Fig. 21.

CIRCLES. &c.

Fig. 22.

Fig. 23.

Arc

Chord

Fig. 24.

Radius   Radius

Arc

Fig. 25.

E   F

PRELIMINARY EXERCISES,

To accustom the student to the mode of handling the compasses, set squares, &c.

1. Having provided himself with the necessary instruments and a sheet of paper (at least four times as large as the page of this book), secured to the drawing-board by pins, the student should commence by making an enlarged copy of Fig. 1* in the following manner:—

With the H pencil, and along the edge of the T-square or straight-edge, draw a horizontal line, as A B, across the paper. Then take a distance, say 1 inch, in the pencil compasses, and, placing the steel point on the line, describe the first circle, taking care to hold the compasses as near the top as possible. Then place the steel point on C, that is, where the first circle cuts the straight line, and describe the part of the second circle as shown. And so on till the other extremity of the line is reached. Now describe the small circle (radius half the large one) with the same centre E, then the small arc with centre C, and so on to the end.

2. This exercise, similar to the last, had best be begun by marking off, with the dividers, the points 1, 2, 3, 4, &c., at a distance half an inch apart. Next describe all the small circles with ½-inch radius. Then the larger arcs with 1-inch radius.

3. In this exercise, begin by drawing the lower horizontal line and stepping off on it a number of equal divisions, each ½ an inch. Then place the set-square on the T-square in this manner and draw the perpendicular through O. Mark off the distances 1, 2, 3, 4, 5 on it, each ½ inch. The long lines may then be drawn through these points by the aid of the T-square, and the short perpendicular ones by the aid of the set-square placed upon it. The strong lines should then be put in with the HB or F pencil.

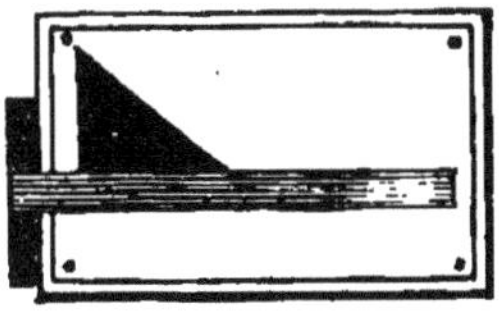

4. This is a similar exercise: the diagonal lines being drawn along the hypotenuse of the angle, or set-square of 45°, instead of the perpendicular edge as above.

* All the exercises and problems should be drawn much larger than the examples here given (at least twice the dimensions). These figures have been constructed on a small scale so that they might be placed within the compass of these pages.

Fig. 1.

A
E
C
B

Fig. 2.

1
2
3
4
5
6
7
8
9
10
11
12
13

Fig. 3.

5
4
3
2
1
0
1
2
3
4
5
6
7
8
9
10
11
12
13

Fig. 4

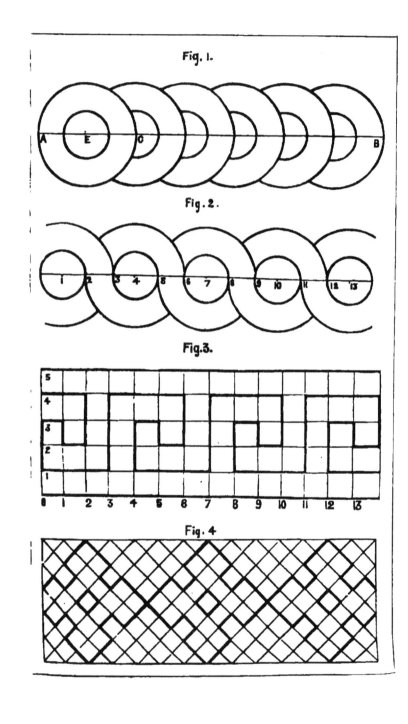

LESSON I.—**THE CONSTRUCTION OF RECTILINEAL FIGURES FROM GIVEN SIDES.**

"All straight lines drawn from the centre to the circumference of a circle are equal."—*Euclid* i. def. 30.

Problem 1.—*To construct an equilateral triangle on a given base* A B.

With centre A and radius A B describe the arc B C; with centre B and the same radius describe the arc A C to intersect the former in C. Draw the straight lines C A and C B.

Note.—The lines of the required figure are to be made stronger than the construction lines.

Problem 2.—*To construct an isosceles triangle, the base* D E *and one of the equal sides* F G *being given.*

With centre D and radius F G describe an arc; with centre E and the same radius describe another to intersect it in H. Draw lines H D and H E.

Note.—If another isosceles triangle equal to this were constructed on D E below it, the resulting figure would be a rhombus. Hence—

Problem 3.—*To construct a rhombus, the diagonal* J K *and one side* L M *being given.*

With centre J and radius L M describe an arc above and below the line J K. With centre K and the same radius describe an arc to intersect it in O and P. Draw lines O J, O K, P J, and P K.

Problem 4.—*To construct any triangle, its three sides* O P, Q R, *and* S T *being given.*

With centre O and radius Q R describe an arc; with centre P and radius S T describe another to intersect it in V. Draw the lines V O and V P.

Note.—If the same figure be constructed on the other side of O P, that is, below it, the result will be a trapezion, as shown in Fig. 4 *a*; or a parallelogram, as shown in 4 *b*. Hence we may construct a parallelogram or a trapezion, given the diagonal and the two unequal sides.

Problem 5.—*To construct a polygon equal to a given one* A B C D E.

Divide the figure into triangles by drawing diagonals A C and A D. Construct a triangle equal to A B C (Prob. 4). On the side equal to A C construct a triangle equal to A D C. On the side equal to A D construct a triangle equal to A E D.

Note.—It is not necessary that the diagonals should actually be drawn in practice; the *length* of the diagonal is all that is needed to describe the intersecting arc : its position may be imagined.

On page 85 the student will find six exercises on these problems, which he is recommended to work before proceeding further. He is strongly advised to adopt this plan of study after each of the lessons, the exercises on which bear the same Roman numerals as the lessons themselves.

Fig. 1.

C
A
B

Fig 2.

H
D
E
F
G

Fig. 3.

O
J
K
P
L
M

Fig. 4.

V
P
O
Q
R
S
T

Fig. 4a

Fig. 4b

Fig. 5.

D
E
C
A
B

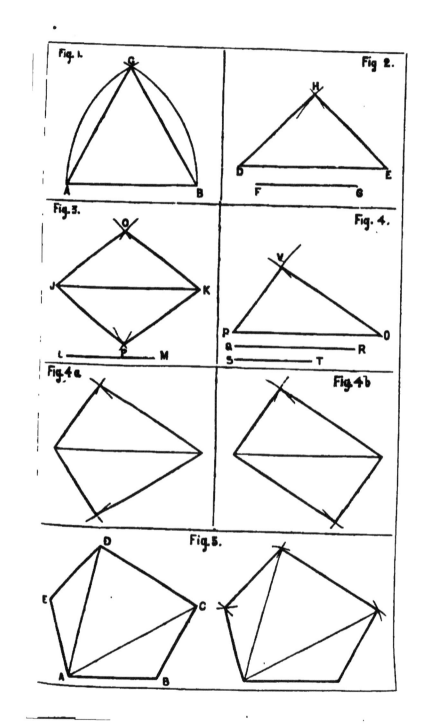

LESSON II.—**THE BISECTION OF LINES AND ANGLES.**

"The straight line which joins the vertices of two isosceles triangles on opposite sides of the same base, bisects the base and each of the vertical angles."

Problem 6.—*To bisect a given line* Q R, *that is, to divide it into two equal parts.*

With centre Q, and any radius greater than half the line, describe an arc above and below the line. With centre R and the same radius intersect it in S and T. Draw the line S T.

Note.—The student will easily see that this construction is identical with that of Prob. 3.

An arc may be bisected in the same manner.
If we bisect each of these parts, as in Fig. 6 a, we have the line divided into four equal parts. By again bisecting each of these, the line would thus be divided into eight equal parts, and so on for sixteen, thirty-two, &c.

Note.—The line S T bisects Q R *perpendicularly;* hence—

Problem 7.—*To draw a perpendicular to a given line* A B *from a given point* C *in it.*

With centre C and any radius mark off C X and C Z equal to each other. With centres X and Z, and any radius greater than half of X Z, describe arcs to intersect in W. Join C and W.

Problem 8.—*To draw a perpendicular to a given line* C H *from a point* K *outside it.*

With K as centre and any radius describe an arc to intersect the line in two points L and M. With centres L and M and any radius, but the same in both cases, describe arcs to intersect as in N. Draw the line K N.

Problem 9.—*To bisect a given angle* ‾A B C.

With centre B and any radius describe an arc to cut the lines in D and E. With centres D and E and any radius describe arcs to intersect as in F. Draw the line B F. If we bisect each of these angles as in Fig. 9 a, we have the given angle divided into four equal parts. And by continuing the same process, the angle may be divided into eight, sixteen, thirty-two, &c., equal parts.

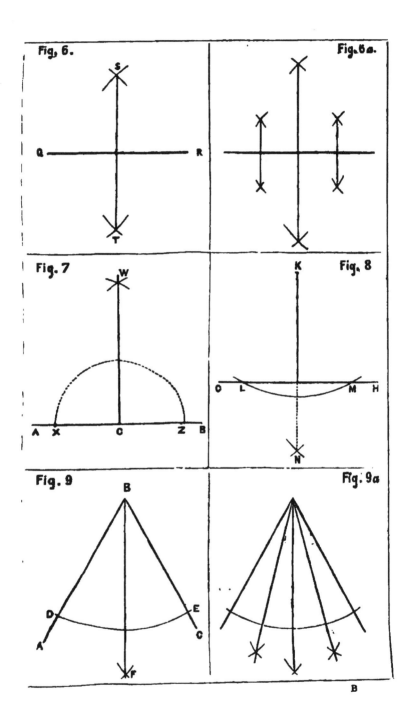

Fig, 6.

S

Q ———————— R

T

Fig, 6a.

Fig. 7

W

A X   C   Z B

Fig, 8

K

G L   M H

N

Fig. 9

B

D   E
        C
A

F

Fig. 9a

B

LESSON III.—**THE CONSTRUCTION OF RECTILINEAL FIGURES FROM GIVEN SIDES AND ANGLES.**

"In equal circles, equal arcs have equal chords."—*Euclid* iii. 29.

Problem 10.—*To make an angle equal to a given one* A B C.

Draw any line K E. With centre B and any radius describe the arc F G. With centre K and the same radius describe the arc H D. With distance F G as radius and H as centre cut the arc in R. Draw from K through R.

Problem 11.—*To construct a triangle, two sides* M N *and* O P *and the contained angle* Q *being given.*

At M with the line M N make an angle equal to the given one Q. Cut off a part M R equal to O P. Draw R N.

Problem 12.—*To construct an isosceles triangle, one of the equal sides* A B *and one of the equal angles* E *being given.*

At A make with the line A B an angle B A F equal to E. With centre B and radius B A describe an arc to cut A F in G. Join G and B.

Problem 13.—*To construct a triangle, the base* S T *and the angles* V *and* W *at the base being given.*

At S make an angle equal to V ; at T make an angle equal to W. Produce the lines till they meet in X.

Problem 14.—*On a given line* H K *to construct a triangle similar to a given one* Z M N.

At H make with the line H K an angle equal to the angle at Z. At K make an angle equal to the angle at M. Produce the lines till they meet in O. The angle at O will be equal to the angle at N ; for the three angles of every triangle are equal to two right angles.—*Euclid* i. 32 cor.

Problem 15.—*To construct an isosceles triangle, the base* F G *and the vertical angle* H *being given.*

With centre H and any radius cut the lines in K and J. Draw K J. At F and G make an angle equal to H K J. Produce the lines to meet in M.

Problem 16.—*On a given base* F G *to construct a polygon similar to a given one* E H J K L.

Draw the diagonals E J and E K. At F make the three angles G F M, M F N, and N F O each equal respectively to the angles H E J, J E K, and K E L. Make the angle F G M equal to E H J; and F M N equal to E J K; and, lastly, F N O equal to E K L.

Fig. 10

C
A
B
D
F
O
R
K
H
E

Fig. 11

Q
R
M
N
O
P

Fig. 12

G
E
A
B

Fig. 13.

X
V
W
S
T

Fig. 14

N
Z
M
O
N
K

Fig. 15

M
H
K
J
F
G

Fig. 16.

K
L
J
E
H
N
O
M
F
G

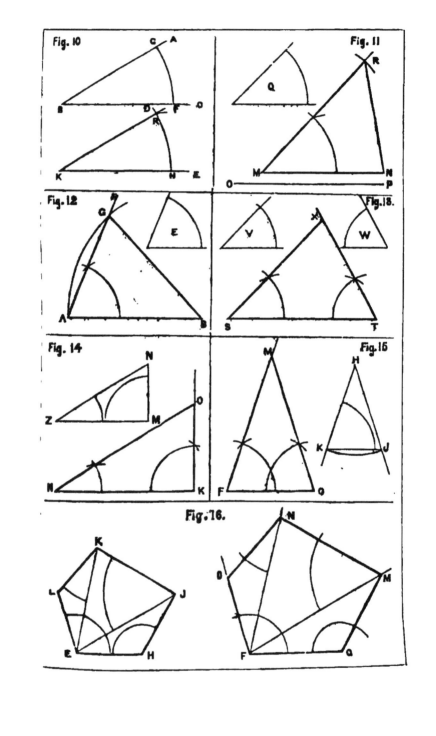

Lesson IV.—RIGHT ANGLES AND RECTANGULAR FIGURES.

" The angle in a semicircle is a right angle."—*Euclid* iii. 31.

Problem 17.—*To draw a perpendicular to a given line* A B *from a given point* C *within it.*

Take any point X nearer to C than to A. With centre X and radius X C describe arc Y C X. From the intersection Y draw a line through X to meet the arc in Z. Draw Z C.

Problem 18.—*To draw a perpendicular to a given line* D E *from a given point* F *outside it.*

From F draw any line F P to meet D E. Bisect F P in R, and describe the semicircle F S P. Draw line from F to intersection S.

Problem 19.—*To construct a right-angled triangle, its hypotenuse* G H *and one side* I K *being given.*

Bisect G H in Q, and describe a semicircle on it. With radius I K and centre G cut the semicircle in T. Draw T G, T H.

Problem 20.—*To construct a right-angled triangle, its hypotenuse* M N *and one acute angle* L *being given.*

Describe a semicircle on M N. At M make an angle M N P equal to the given one L. Join the intersection P with N.

Problem 21.—*To construct a square on a given line* O P.

At O erect a perpendicular to O P (Prob. 17). Cut off O M equal to O P. With M and P as centres and radius O P describe arcs to intersect in N. Draw M N, N P.

Problem 22.—*To construct an oblong, two unequal sides* Q R *and* S T *being given.*

At Q erect a perpendicular to Q R. Make Q G equal to S T. With centre R and radius S T describe an arc. With centre G and radius Q R describe another to intersect in H. Draw G H, H R.

Problem 23.—*To construct a square, the diagonal* V W *being given.*

Bisect V W by perpendicular in F. With centre F and radius F W describe arcs to cut the perpendicular in D and E. Join points V D W E.

Problem 24.—*To construct an oblong or rectangle, one diagonal* O X *and one side* Y Z *being given.*

Bisect O X in A. With centre A and radius A O describe the circle O C X B. With radius Y Z and centres O and X cut the circle in C and B. Draw O C, C X, X B, B O.

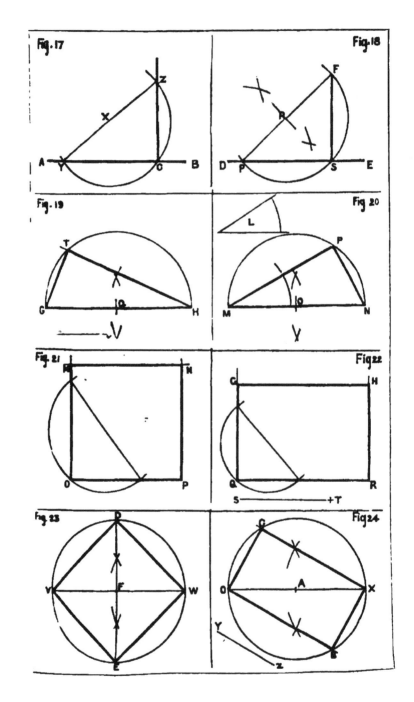

Fig. 17

Z
X
A
Y
C
B

Fig. 18

F
D
P
S
E

Fig. 19

T
G
Q
H

Fig. 20

L
P
M
O
N

Fig. 21

N
O
P

Fig. 22

G
H
Q
R
S
T

Fig. 23

D
F
W
E

Fig. 24

C
O
A
X
Y
Z

LESSON V.—ON PARALLELS.
" If a straight line fall upon two parallel straight lines, it makes the alternate angles equal."—*Euclid* i. 29.

Problem 25.—*To draw a line parallel to a given straight line* H J *at a given distance* K L.
With radius K L and any points B and C in the line as centres describe arcs on the same side of H J. Draw a line to touch these arcs.*

Problem 26.—*Through a given point* C *to draw a line parallel to a given straight line* A B.
With any point L as centre, and radius L C, describe arc C M. With centre C and same radius describe arc L N O. Cut off L N equal to C M. Draw C N.

Problem 27.—*Through a given point* F *to draw a line meeting a given line* D E *at an angle equal to a given one* G.
Through F draw F H parallel to D E. At F make the angle H F K equal to the given angle G. Then F K E will also be equal to it.

Problem 28.—*To draw a line bisecting the angle made by two lines* M N *and* O P *without using the apex.*
Draw A Z parallel to O P ; at the same distance draw Z Y parallel to M N to intersect in Z. Bisect the angle A Z Y.

Problem 29.—*To construct an isosceles triangle, given the altitude* Q R *and one of the equal angles* S.
Through Q and R draw lines at right angles to Q R. At Q make angles T Q L and V Q M each equal to S. Produce the lines to meet W X.

Problem 30.—*To construct an equilateral triangle, given the altitude* A B.
Through A and B draw lines at right angles to A B. With centre A and any radius describe semicircle C G H D. From C and D with same radius mark points G and H. Draw A G and A H, and produce to meet E F.

Problem 31.—*To construct a triangle, given the base* V W, *the angle* X *at the vertex, and the angle* Y *at the base.*
At V make the angle W V K equal to Y, and the angle K V J equal to X. Draw W K parallel to V J.

Problem 32.—*To construct a triangle, given its perimeter* A B *and two of its angles* C *and* D.
At A make an angle equal to C ; at B an angle equal to D. Bisect the angles at A and B. Through the intersection H draw H E parallel to G A, and H F parallel to G B.

* *Note.*—This method is slightly defective, though it is universally practised. The line is a tangent to the two curves, and the tangent points should first be found. They can be found by erecting perpendiculars at B and C.

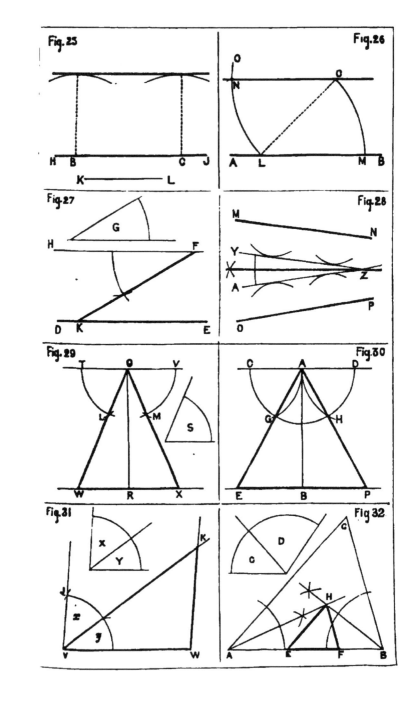

Fig. 25

H B   C J

K —————— L

Fig. 26

O

N   O

A L   M B

Fig. 27

G

H   F

D K   E

Fig. 28

M   N

Y   Z

A

O   P

Fig. 29

T Q V

L   M   S

W R X

Fig. 30

C A D

G   H

E B P

Fig. 31

X

Y

J   K

x

y

V   W

Fig 32

C

D

c

H

A E F B

Lesson VI.—PROPORTIONALS.

" If a straight line be parallel to one side of a triangle, it cuts the other sides, or those produced, proportionally."—*Euclid* vi. 2.

Problem 33.—*To divide a line* A B *into any number of equal parts (say five).*

Draw A X at any angle with A B. From A step any distance five times on the line A X. Join 5 and B. Through 4, 3, 2, and 1 draw parallels to 5 B to cut A B.

Problem 34.—*To divide a line* C D *proportionally to a given divided line* E F.

Draw C W at any angle with C D. Transfer the divisions E R, R S, S F, to the line C W. Join *f* and D. Draw parallels to *f* D through *s* and *r*.

Problems 35 and 36.—*To find a fourth proportional (greater or less) to three given lines* A B, A C, A D.

Draw two lines at any angle with each other. From *a*, step off the distance A B on one of the lines, and A C on the other line. Join *b* and *c*. Then mark off the distance A D on the same line with *a b* (the first term). Through *d* draw *d x* parallel to *b c;* then *a x* is the fourth proportional. That is, A B is to A C as A D is to *a x.*

Problems 37 and 38.—*To find a third proportional (greater or less) to two given lines* E F *and* E G.

That is, to find a fourth proportional to three given lines, two of which are equal. (E F : E G : : E G : the required line.) Proceed as in the previous case. Place the first and third terms E F and E G on the same line, and the second, E G, on the other. Join 1st and 2d, i.e., *f* and *g;* and through the third, *g*, draw *g x* parallel to *f g;* then *e x* is the third proportional.

Problem 39.—*To find a mean proportional to two given lines* A B *and* B C.

Place them in the same straight line A C. On A C describe a semicircle. At B erect a perpendicular to meet the arc in D. Then A B : B D : : B D : B C.—*Euclid* vi. 13.

Note.—The dotted lines are drawn merely to show the connection this problem has with the theory of similar triangles.

Problem 40.—*To divide a line* E F *into extreme and mean ratio.*

Bisect E F in M. At E erect a perpendicular E G equal to E M. Join G and F. Make G H equal to G E. With centre F and radius F H describe arc H K to cut the line E F in K ; then E K : K F : : K F : E F.—*Euclid* vi. 30, and ii. 11.

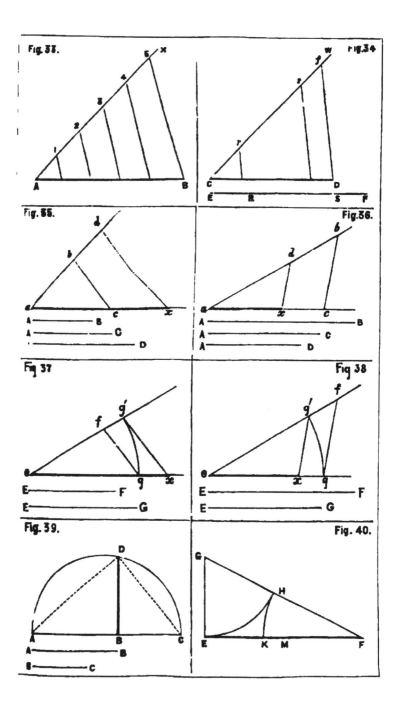

Fig. 33.

A
B
1
2
3
4
5
x

Fig. 34

C
D
E
R
S
F
r
s
f
w

Fig. 35.

a
b
d
c
x
A B
A C
D

Fig. 36.

a
d
b
x
c
A B
A C
A D

Fig 37

f
g′
q
x
E F
E G

Fig 38

g′
f
x
q
E F
E G

Fig. 39.

D
A
B
C
A B
B C

Fig. 40.

G
H
E
K
M
F

LESSON VII.—**THE APPLICATION OF PROPORTION TO THE CONSTRUCTION OF PLANE SCALES.**

It is frequently necessary to make the drawings of objects larger or smaller than the objects themselves. The plan of a house, for instance, cannot conveniently be drawn as large as the house itself. It suffices for all practical purposes, however, if the drawing preserves the same ratio in its parts as the original does. To enable us to make a reduced or enlarged drawing a *scale* is used. Suppose we wish our drawing to be $\frac{1}{12}$ the size of the original, a distance of 1 foot on the object would be represented by 1 inch on the drawing. On the scale or rule used in this case, the inches would represent feet; and if each inch were divided into twelve equal parts, each part would represent $\frac{1}{12}$ of a foot, that is, 1 inch. A B is a scale of 1 inch to 1 foot, or $\frac{1}{12}$ of the actual size. C D is a scale of 1 inch to 1 yard, or $\frac{1}{36}$ of the actual size.

Problem 41.—*To construct a scale of $\frac{3}{4}$ of an inch to the foot, or $\frac{1}{16}$, to show feet and inches.*

Mark off a number of divisions each $\frac{3}{4}$ of an inch on the line E F. Each of these will represent a foot. Divide one of them into twelve equal parts and number them as shown in the figure.

Note.—When very minute divisions are required a *diagonal scale* is used.

Problem 42.—*To construct a diagonal scale of 1 inch to 1 yard, or $\frac{1}{36}$, to show feet and inches.*

Draw the line X Y. From X mark off X 2 equal to 1 inch. Divide it into three equal parts. Each of these parts will represent a foot. Erect a perpendicular at X and mark off on it twelve equal divisions. Draw parallels to X Y through them. Erect a perpendicular at 0, 1, 2, 3, 4, &c. Draw diagonal from 0 to 12. Then A B represents $\frac{1}{12}$ of a foot or 1 inch, C D = 2 ft. 2 in., E F = 3 ft. 7 in., V W = 5 ft. 11 in.

Note.—It will be seen that this construction is based upon the principle of similar triangles.

Problem 43.—*To construct a diagonal scale to show $\frac{1}{100}$ of 1 inch.*

Draw a line G H. Mark off G O equal to 1 inch. Erect a perpendicular at G. Mark off ten equal divisions on it. Through each draw parallels to G H. At O erect perpendicular O C. Divide O G and C K each into ten equal parts. Draw 9 K and parallels to it through 8, 7, 6, &c. Then L M = 1 $\frac{1}{100}$ in. or 1.01 in., N P = 1.03 in., Q R = 1.16 in., S T = 2.69 in.

INCHES
FEET
A
B
FEET
YARDS
C
D
E
F

Fig.41.

Fig.42.

W
V
F
E
D
C
A
X
Y

Fig.43

K
C
T
S
G
P
N
L
G
H

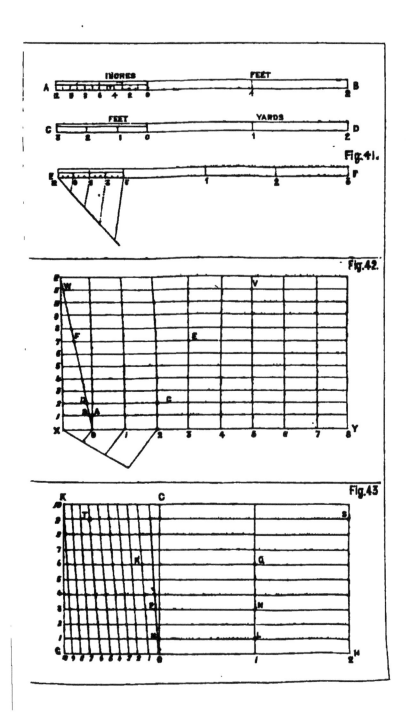

LESSON VIII.—THE CIRCLE AND ITS DIVISIONS.

If a right angle or a quadrant be divided into 90 equal parts, each part is called a degree. A semicircle therefore contains 180 degrees, and a circle 360 degrees.

Problem 44.—*To divide a given circle into four equal parts.*
Draw two diameters at right angles to each other as A B and C D.

Problem 45.—*To divide a given circle into eight equal parts.*
Proceed as in Prob. 44 ; then bisect each of the four right angles at the centre by diameters E F and G H.

Problem 46.—*To divide a given circle into six equal parts.*
Draw diameter I K. With centres I and K, radius I L, mark off I M, I N, K O, K P.

Problem 47.—*To divide a given circle into twelve equal parts.*
Draw two diameters at right angles as Q R and S T. With centres Q, T, R, and S, and radius S Z, describe arcs to cut the circumference.

Note.—By joining the points of section as indicated by the dotted lines, the following regular figures may be inscribed in a circle : 1. a square, 2. an octagon, 3. a hexagon and equilateral triangle, 4. a dodecagon.

Problem 48.—*To trisect a right angle* X V Y.
With centre V and any radius describe the quadrant U W. With centres W and U and same radius cut the arcs in A and B. Draw V A and V B.

Problem 49.—*To construct a scale of chords.*
Describe the quadrant C D E and trisect it (Prob 48.) in points 3 and 6. Divide each third into three equal parts by trial. Each part measures an angle of 10°. Draw the chord C E and transfer the distances E 1, E 2, E 3, &c., on the arc to the chord. Number them 10, 20, 30, &c.

Problem 50.—*To construct an angle of a given magnitude (say 40°) by scale of chords.*
Draw the line F G. Take the distance o to 60 (in all cases) as radius (for this is the radius used in constructing the scale), and with centre G describe the arc H J. Take o to 40° and mark off H N. Join G and N.

Note.—The *Protractor* is also used for measuring and making angles. It is generally semicircular in shape and is divided into 180 equal parts, each of which is one degree. To construct an angle of 50°, for example, place the centre of the base of the protractor upon point G and the base upon F G. Mark a point on the paper at 50°. Join G and the point.

Problem 51.—*To divide the circumference of a circle into any number of equal parts (say five), and hence to inscribe any regular polygon in a circle.*
Draw a diameter J K. Divide it into five equal parts (Prob. 33). With centres J and K, radius J K, describe arcs to intersect in N. From N draw through division 2 (in all cases) and produce to M. The arc J M is ⅕. Step it round on the rest of the circumference. Join the points to construct the inscribed figure.

Note.—This general method for dividing a circle into any number of equal parts, though not based on theoretical principles, is useful in practice, giving a very close approximation to accuracy.

Fig 44

C
A
B
D

Fig 4[5]

E
G
H
F

Fig 46

I
N
M
L
P
O
K

Fig 47

Q
S
Z
T
R

Fig 48

X
U
30°
A
30°
B
30°
V
W
Y

Fig 49

1 2 3 4 5 6 7 8 9
C
D
E
10 20 30 40 50 60 70 80

Fig 50

J
N
40°
F
H
G

Fig 51

N
J
1 2 3 4 5
K
M

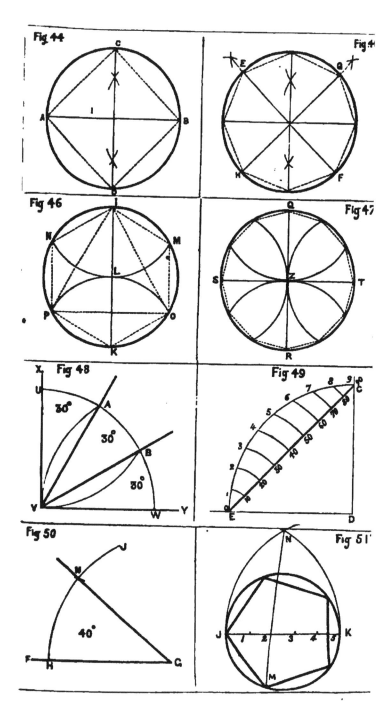

LESSON IX.—THE USE OF SCALES IN THE CONSTRUCTION OF IRREGULAR POLYGONS.

Problem 52.—*To construct an irregular polygon, given the following*:—

Sides. A B = 1 $\frac{5}{8}''$, B C = 1 $\frac{3}{8}''$, C D = 1 $\frac{3}{4}''$, D E = 1 $\frac{1}{8}''$.

Angles. A B C = 110°, B C D = 100°, C D E = 105°.

First make a rough freehand sketch of the polygon as shown. This will enable us to see the relative position of the sides and angles. Then draw a line A B equal to 1 $\frac{5}{8}$. At B make the angle A B C equal 110°, either with protractor or scale of chords. Make B C equal to 1 $\frac{3}{8}$. At C make the angle B C D 100°. Make C D equal to 1 $\frac{3}{4}$. At D make an angle 105°. Cut off D E equal to 1 $\frac{1}{8}$, and join E and A.

Problem 53.—*To construct an irregular polygon, given the following*:—

Sides. A B = 1.88″, B C = 1.63″, C D = 1.05″, D E = 1.12″, A F = 1.09″.

Diagonals. A C = 2.68″, A D = 2.57″, A E = 2.26″, B F = 2.6.″

Make a rough freehand sketch as before. We can readily see now that the work is but another form of Problem 5, the only difference being that the sides of the triangles are given in numbers instead of actual lines. Draw A B = 1.88″. With centre B and radius B C, equal to 1.63″, describe an arc; with centre A and radius A C, 2.68″, describe another to intersect it. This gives point C. Join B and C. With centre C and radius C D, 1.05″, describe an arc; and with centre A and radius A D, 2.57″, describe another to intersect it in D. Join C and D. The other points may be found in the same manner.

Problem 54.—*To construct a polygon* V W X Y Z, *given the following*:—*A point* C *within the polygon.*

Lines. C V = 1.3″, C W = 1.4″, C X = 1.42″, C Y = 1.92″, C Z = 1.93.

Angles. V C W = 95°, W C X = 75°, X C Y = 65°, Y C Z = 35°.

After having made a rough sketch as in Fig. 54, the student will find no difficulty in constructing the figure accurately.

Problem 55.—*To construct a polygon, given the following*:—

Sides. K L = 1.75″, K O = 1.76″.

Diagonals. K M = 2.66″, K N = 2.22″.

Angles. L K M = 30°, M K N = 60°, N K O = 20°.

Proceed as before, and work out the result by applying the principles taught in the construction of triangles.

Note.—These problems, together with those in the next lesson, illustrate no new principles; they are, strictly speaking, merely exercises on the use of plane scales, the diagonal scale, and scale of chords.

Fig. 52.

d
105°
e
c
100°
110°
a
b
D
C
E
A
B

Fig. 53

e
d
f
c
a
b
E
D
C
F
A
B

Fig. 54.

X
W
75°
65°
Y
35°
C
95°
Z
V

Fig. 55

N
O
M
60°
K
L

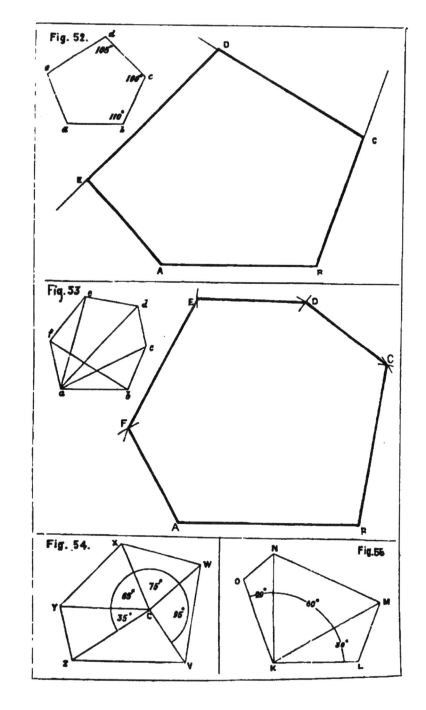

Lesson X.—THE USE OF SCALES IN PATTERN DRAWING.

Problem 56.—*To make a finished geometrical drawing to any required scale (say ⅛ of an inch to 1 foot) from a sketch, the dimensions being given in figures.*

> Draw the centre line A B. Make it 7 feet long by scale, for this is the length given in the sketch. The breadth is to be 3 feet. Through the extremities A and B draw the horizontal lines C D and E F, and measure off 1½ feet from A and B on each side. Draw the perpendiculars C E and D F. The position of the perpendicular lines of the panels may be found in the same way, by measuring from the sides or centre line the distances given in the sketch. Then measure off the width of the bottom rail (8″) from B on the centre line and draw a parallel to the base. Then another parallel 1′ 9″ above it ; then another 8″ from that, and lastly one 4″ from the top. All these lines should be kept very faint, to allow those portions which form part of the required figure to appear distinctly when drawn with a blacker line.

Problem 57.—*To make an enlarged copy of a drawing, say 1½ times the size, or to the scale of ¾.*

> Construct a proportional scale of ¾ by drawing lines A B and B C at any angle with each other, and measuring off from B on one of them any convenient distance *twice*, and on the other the same distance *three times*. Join 2 and 3. Mark off any number of divisions on B A, and through them draw parallels to 2, 3. The divisions on B C will be 1½ times the size of those on B A. Find the length of the centre line Y Z on B A. It is B X. Then B W (the corresponding division on B C) gives the length of the centre line of the enlarged drawing required. The width and every other measurement can be found in the same manner.

Note.—The curves at the top are described with the centre Z.

Problem 58.—*To make a reduced copy of a drawing, say to the scale of ⅔.*

> This differs from the preceding problem only in the use of the scale. The dimensions of the given figure are applied to the *longer* line, and the corresponding divisions on the short one give the required dimensions of the copy.

Fig. 56

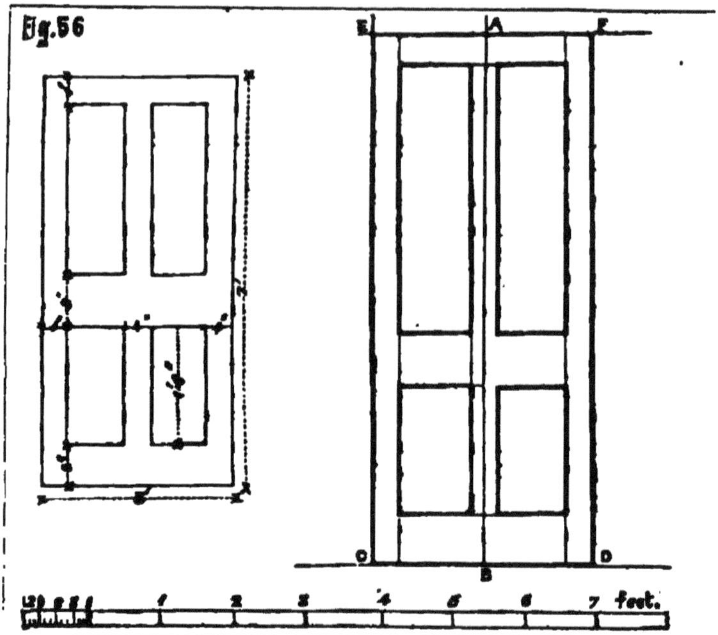

E
A
F
C
D
B
1 2 3 4 5 6 7 feet.

Fig. 57

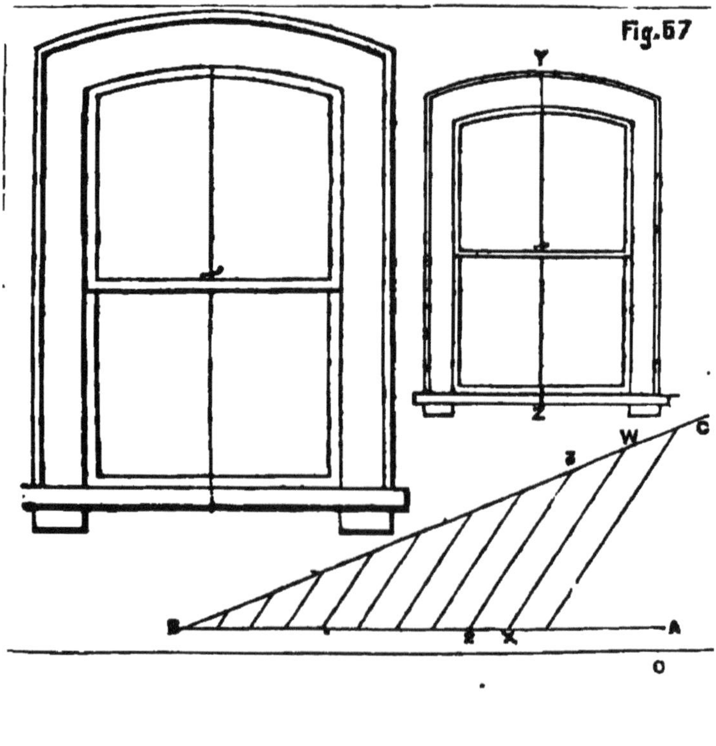

Y
Z
W
C
B
X
A
O

LESSON XI.—CIRCLES TO PASS THROUGH GIVEN POINTS.

"A straight line which bisects a chord of a circle at right angles passes through the centre of the circle."—*Euclid* iii. 1, *Corollary.*

Problem 59.—*To find the centre of a given circle.*

Draw any two chords A B and B C making angles with each other. Bisect them by perpendiculars. The intersection of these perpendiculars is the centre.

Problem 60.—*To complete the circle, an arc of which is given,* E G F H.

Draw any two chords and bisect them by perpendiculars. The intersection of these perpendiculars is the centre, and the distance from it to E, G, H, or F is the radius.

Problem 61.—*To describe a circle to pass through three given points* K L M, *which are not in a straight line.*

Join K L, L M. Bisect the lines, and proceed as above.

Problem 62.—*To describe a circle about a given triangle* P Q R.

Bisect any two sides by perpendiculars. Proceed as above.

Problem 63.—*One side* A B *and one angle* (108°) *of a regular polygon being given, to complete it.*

At A or B make the required angle. Make A C equal to A B. Bisect A B and A C by perpendiculars. With the intersection E as centre and E A or E B as radius describe a circle. Step the distance A B or A C on the remaining part of the circumference, and join the points.

Problem 64.—*To construct any regular polygon, given one of its sides* F G.

With centre F or G and radius G F describe a semicircle on F G produced. Divide the semicircle into as many equal parts as the required figure has sides—say a heptagon—then seven parts. From G draw through 2d division. Then F G 2 is one angle of the figure. Proceed as in last problem.

Problem 65.—*To construct a regular hexagon, given one of its sides* J K. (Special method.)

With centres J and K and radius J K describe arcs to intersect in M. Describe a circle, centre M, radius M J. Step the distance J K round on the circumference and join the points.

Problem 66.—*To construct a regular hexagon, given the diagonal* N O.

Bisect N O in R. Describe a circle, centre R, radius R N. From N and O step the radius on the circumference above and below. Join the points.

Fig. 59

B
D
C
A

Fig 60

F
G
H
E

Fig. 61.

L
M
K

Fig. 62

Q
P
R

Fig. 63

C
E
108°
A
B

Fig. 64

4
3
5
2
6
1
7
F
G

Fig. 65

M
J
K

Fig. 66

N
O
R

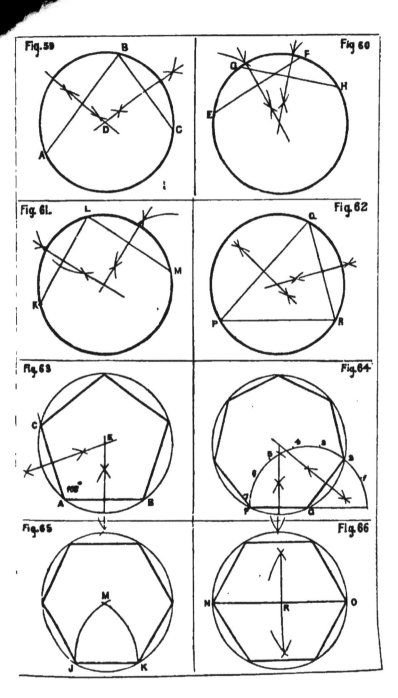

Lesson XII.—TANGENTS TO CIRCLES.

"The straight line which is drawn at right angles to the diameter of a circle from its extremity is a tangent."—*Euclid* iii. 16, *Corollary.*

Problem 67.—*To draw a tangent to a circle through any point A in the circumference.*

Draw the radius A B.   At A erect a perpendicular A C to A B. A C is the tangent.

Problem 68.—*To construct a regular polygon about a given circle.*

Divide the circle into the same number of parts that the required figure has sides (say six).   Through each of the points of division draw tangents.

Problem 69.—*To draw a tangent to a circle from a given point E outside it.*

Join E with centre F.   Construct a semicircle on F E.   From E draw a line through the intersection G.

Note.—By describing a semicircle on the other side of F E, another tangent may be drawn.

Problem 70.—*To draw a common tangent to two equal circles.*

1st. Join the centres H and J.   At H and J erect perpendiculars H N and J O to the line H J.   Draw a line through N and O.

2d. Bisect H J in K.   On H K describe a semicircle.   Join H with the intersection L.   Draw J M parallel to H L.   Draw a line through L and M.

Note.—The first is frequently called an exterior tangent, the second an interior tangent.

Problem 71.—*To draw a tangent to two unequal circles to cross the space between them.*

Join the centres P and Q.   Describe a semicircle on P Q.   Mark R S equal to the radius of the small circle.   With centre P and radius P S describe an arc to cut the semicircle in T. Draw P T, and through Q a parallel Q V to it.   Draw a line through V and W.

Problem 72.—*To draw a tangent to two unequal circles so as not to cross the space between them.*

Join the centres A and B, and describe a semicircle upon it. Mark off H C equal to A D.   With centre B and radius B C describe an arc to cut the semicircle in E.   Join B E and produce to F.   Draw A G parallel to B F.   Draw a line through G and F.

Note.—It will be seen that another tangent could be drawn, both in this and the last problem, by describing a semicircle on the *other* side of the line joining the centres, and proceeding as above.

Fig. 67

A
C
B

Fig. 68

Fig. 69.

E
G
F

Fig. 70.

N
H
K
M
L
O
J

Fig. 71

Q
T
V
W
S
R
P

Fig. 72

G
A
D
H
F
C
E
B

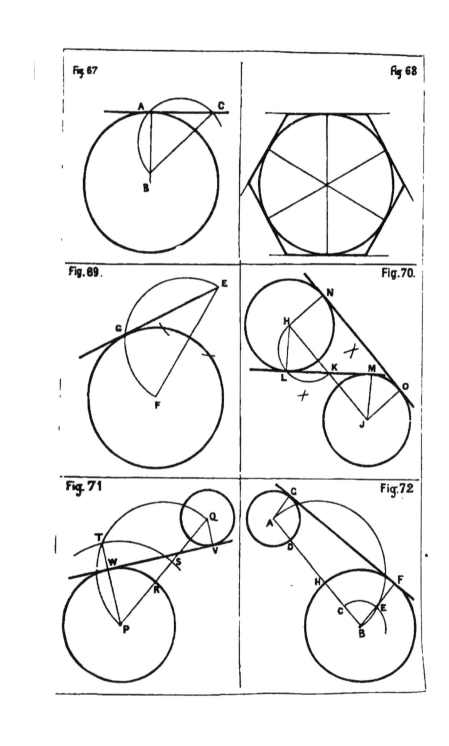

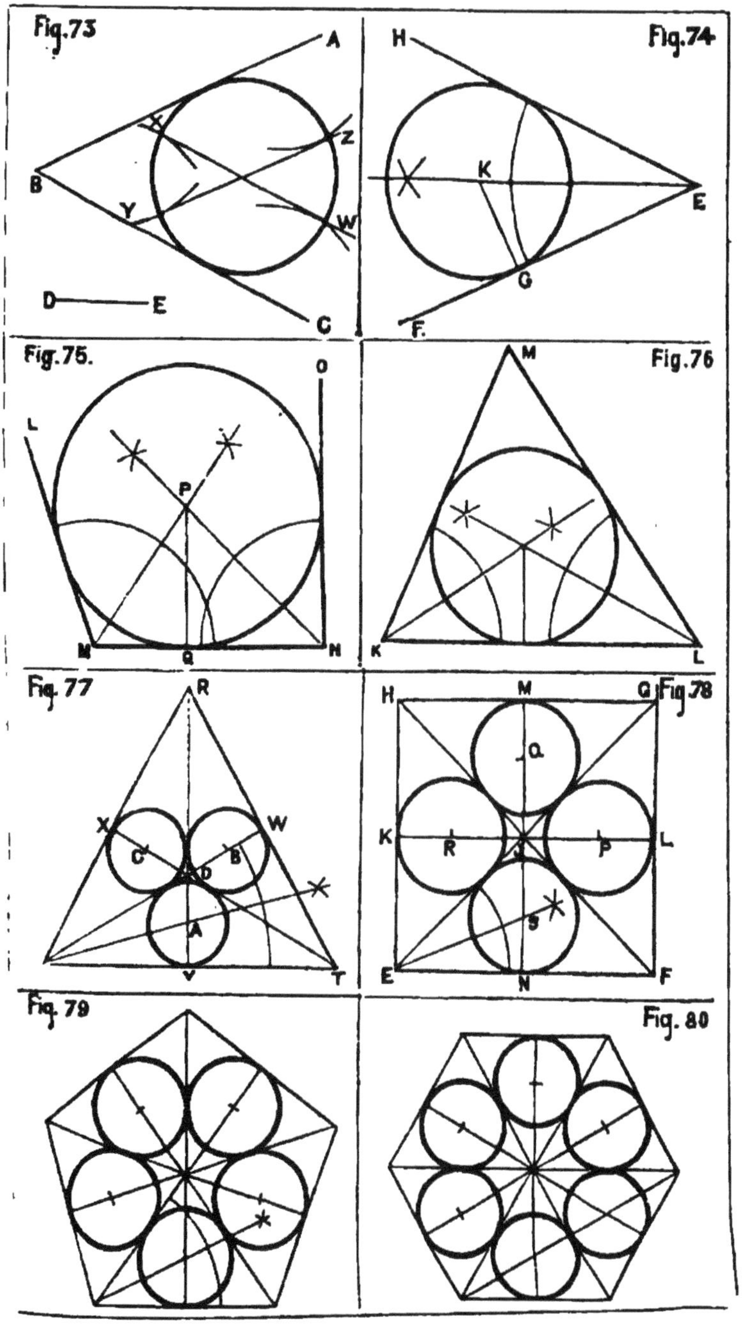
Fig. 73
A
B
C
D
E
Y
Z
W
Fig. 74
H
E
K
G
F.
Fig. 75.
O
L
P
M
Q
N
Fig. 76
M
K
L
Fig. 77
R
X
W
C
B
D
A
V
T
Fig. 78
H
M
G
Q
K
R
P
L
S
E
N
F
Fig. 79
Fig. 80

LESSON XIII.—CIRCLES TO TOUCH STRAIGHT LINES.

"If a straight line be a tangent to a circle, and from the point of contact a line be drawn perpendicular to the tangent, the centre of the circle shall be in that line."—*Euclid* iii. 19.

"If a line drawn from the centre of a circle be perpendicular to the tangent, it will pass through the point of contact."—*Corollary.*

Problem 73.—*To describe a circle of a given radius* D E *to touch two converging lines* A B *and* B C.

Draw W X parallel to C B at a distance equal to D E, and at the same distance draw Y Z parallel to A B. The intersection O is the centre.

Problem 74.—*To describe a circle to touch two converging lines* E F *and* E H, *and to pass through a point* G *in one of them.*

Bisect the angle F E H. From G draw a perpendicular to E F. The intersection K is the centre, K G the radius.

Problem 75.—*To describe a circle to touch three given lines* L M, M N, N O, *making angles with each other.*

Bisect the angles L M N and M N O by lines to intersect in P. From P drop a perpendicular P Q on one of the lines. P is the centre, P Q the radius.

Problem 76.—*To inscribe a circle in a given triangle* K L M.

Bisect two of the angles and proceed as in last problem.

Problem 77.—*In a given equilateral triangle* R S T *to inscribe three equal circles, each to touch one side and two circles.*

Bisect each of the angles. These lines will also bisect the sides in V, W, and X. Inscribe a circle in the triangle D S T (Prob. 76). Mark off D B and D C each equal to D A. Describe the circles with B W and C X as radii.

Problem 78.—*In a given square* E F G H *to inscribe four equal circles, each to touch one side and two circles.*

Draw diagonals E G and H F. Draw diameters K L and M N to bisect the four angles at the centre J. Inscribe a circle in the triangle E J F (Prob. 76). With centre J and radius J S mark off P, Q, and R. These are the centres of the other circles.

Problems 79 and 80.—*In a given regular polygon to inscribe a number of equal circles, each to touch one side and two other circles.*

Divide the figure into equal triangles and inscribe a circle in each, as shown in Problems 77 and 78.

LESSON XIV.—CIRCLES TO TOUCH STRAIGHT LINES—
Continued.

Problem 81.—*To inscribe a circle in a given square* A B C D.

Bisect the angles by drawing the diagonals A C and B D ; then
draw diameters E F and G H.. The intersection J is the
centre and J E the radius.

Problem 82.—*To inscribe within a given square four equal
circles, each to touch two sides and two circles.*

Draw diagonals and diameters as before. Draw K L, K N, M L,
and M N. Join O and P. Then O, P, R, and S are the centres
and O Q is the radius.

Problem 83.—*To inscribe a circle in any regular polygon (say
a pentagon).*

Bisect two of the angles. These lines also bisect the opposite
sides and are perpendicular to them. The intersection T is
the centre, and T V or T W the radius.

Problem 84.—*To inscribe a circle in a rhombus.*

Bisect the angles by drawing diagonals. The intersection X is
the centre. The perpendicular X Y on one of the sides is the
radius.

Problem 85.—*To inscribe a circle in a trapezion.*

Draw the diagonal A B. Bisect one of the other angles. The
intersection C is the centre, and a perpendicular from it on
one of the sides is the radius C D.

Problem 86.—*Within an equilateral triangle to inscribe three
equal circles, each touching two others and two sides of the
triangle.*

Bisect each of the angles by the lines E J, G K, and F H. Inscribe a circle in the trapezion H M J G (Prob. 85). With M
as centre and distance M O, mark off P and Q. These are
the centres of the other two circles.

Problem 87.—*Within a given regular hexagon to inscribe six
equal circles, each touching two others and two sides of the
hexagon.*

Draw the diagonals and diameters. The diameters divide the
figure into six equal trapezions. Inscribe a circle in each.
Proceed as in Problem 86.

Problem 88.—*Within a given regular octagon to inscribe
four equal circles, each touching two others and two sides of the
octagon.*

Draw the diagonals. Then inscribe a circle in the trapezion
R S T V, which is one-fourth of the octagon, and proceed as
before.

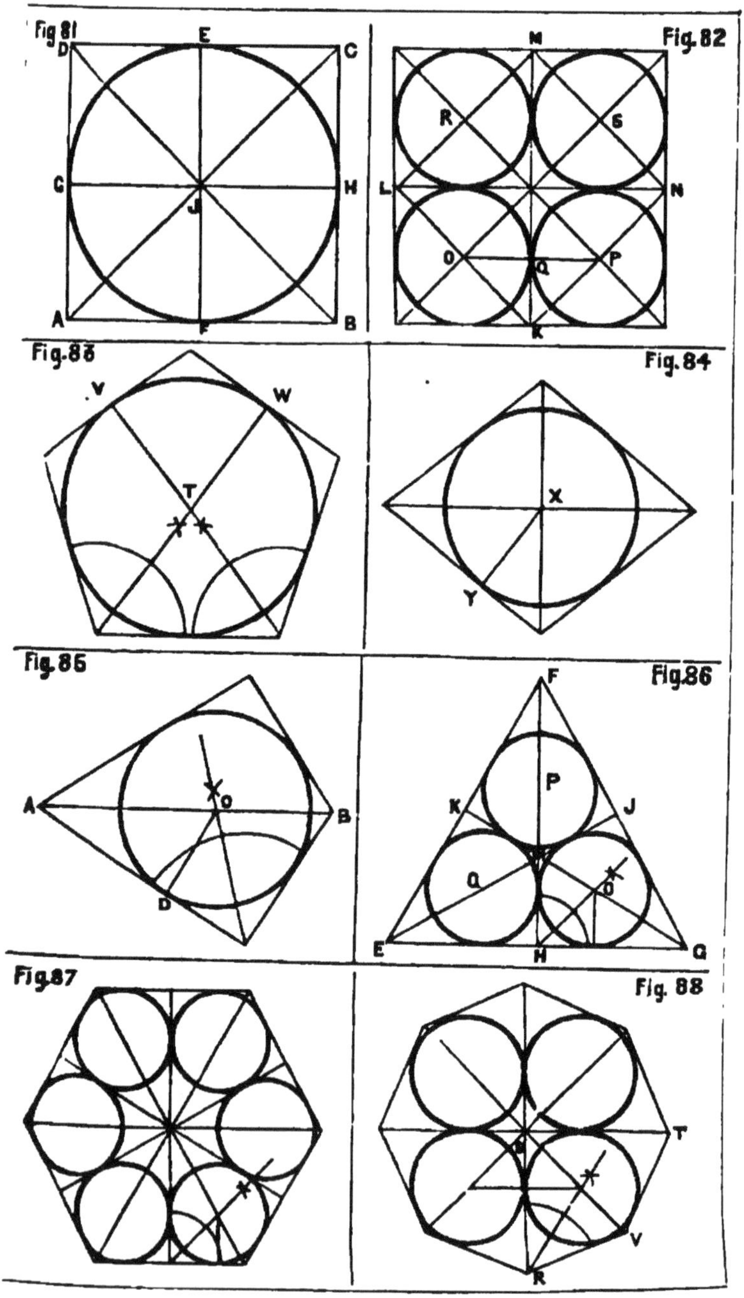
Fig 81
D
E
C
G
H
J
A
F
B
M
Fig. 82
R
S
L
N
O
Q
P
K
Fig. 83
V
W
T
Fig. 84
X
Y
Fig. 85
A
O
B
D
F
Fig. 86
P
K
J
Q
O
E
H
G
Fig. 87
Fig. 88
T
V
R

LESSON XV.—CIRCLES TO TOUCH CIRCLES AND STRAIGHT LINES.

" If two circles touch one another internally, the straight line which joins their centres, being produced, shall pass through the point of contact."—*Euclid* iii. 11.

" If two circles touch one another externally, the straight line which joins their centres shall pass through the point of contact."—*Euclid* iii. 12.

Problem 89.—*To inscribe a circle in a sector* A B C.

Bisect the angles A B C by B D. Through D draw a tangent D E to meet B A produced. Bisect the angle D E B. The intersection F is the centre, and F D the radius.

Problem 90.—*To describe a circle to touch the arc of a sector and the two radii produced.*

Bisect the arc G O by the line H N in K. Through K draw the tangent K L. Bisect the angle K L M by L N. The intersection N is the centre N K the radius.

Problem 91.—*Within a given circle to inscribe any number of equal circles (say four), each to touch two others and the circumference of the given circle.*

Divide the circle into eight (twice four) equal parts by diameters. In the sector P Q R inscribe a circle (Prob. 89). With centre R and radius R S mark off T, V, and W. These points are the centres for the other three circles.

Problem 92.—*About a given circle to describe any number of equal circles (say five), each to touch two others and the circumference of the given one.*

Divide the circle into *five* equal parts in A B C D E. Draw diameters through the points and produce them. Through A draw a tangent to the circle. Bisect the angle A H F. The intersection G is the centre and G A the radius of one of the five circles. From this the centres of the rest will be easily found.

Problem 93.—*To describe a series of circles touching one another and two converging lines* X Y *and* Y Z.

Bisect the angle X Y Z. Take any point A in this line and draw A B perpendicular to Z Y. With centre A and radius A B describe a circle. Through C draw C D a tangent to the circle. Bisect the angle C D Y. This will give E the centre of the next circle, with E C as radius. Through F draw F G parallel to C D, and G H parallel to D E. This gives H the centre of the next circle, and so on for the rest.

Note.—If the part within the tangent points A B C D, Fig. 91, be removed, the result would be a quatrefoil of tangential arcs. A trefoil or a cinquefoil may be inscribed in a circle on the same principle, namely, by first inscribing three or five circles respectively, to touch each other, and omitting the parts within the tangent points. For applications of these problems to geometrical tracery work, see Lesson XXVII.

Fig. 89.

B
F
A
C
D

Fig. 90.

H
G
K
O
L
N
M

Fig. 91

V
A
B
W
T
D
C
S
P
Q

Fig. 92

F
O
H
A
E
B
D
C

Fig. 93

X
A
O
E
F
H
V
G
D
B
Z

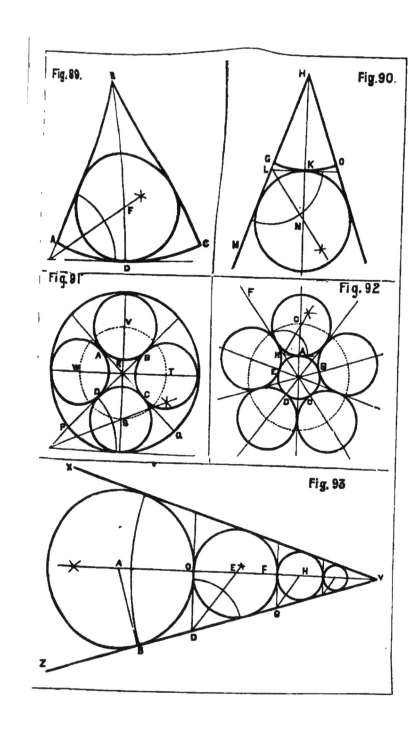

LESSON XVI.—CIRCLES TO TOUCH CIRCLES AND
STRAIGHT LINES—Continued.

Problem 94.—*To describe a circle of a given radius Q to touch
a given circle R and a given line S T.*

Draw V W parallel to S T at a distance equal to Q. With
centre R and a radius equal to that of R and Q together
describe an arc to cut V W in X. This is the centre.

Problem 95.—*To describe a circle to touch a given circle A
and a given straight line E F at a given point B.*

Through B draw a perpendicular to E F. Make B C equal to
the radius of circle A. Join A and C. Bisect A C by a
perpendicular to intersect the other in D. This is the centre
and D B the radius.

Problems 96 and 97.—*To describe a circle to pass through a
given point G, and to touch a given circle H in a given point F.*

Join F and G. Bisect F G by a perpendicular. Join F and
H and produce to meet it in E. This is the centre; E F or
E G the radius.

Problem 98.—*To describe three circles to touch each other, their
radii A, B, and C being given.*

Describe a circle with radius A. From centre D draw a line
D E. Mark off F G equal to B. With centre G describe the
second circle. Mark off F H and F M each equal to C. With
centre D, radius D M, describe an arc. With centre G and
radius G H describe another to intersect in K. This is the
centre of the third circle.

Problem 99.—*Within a given circle to inscribe two others of a
given radii D and E, to touch each other and the circumference
of the given one.*

Draw a diameter L N. Make L O equal to D. With centre O and
radius O L describe a circle. Make P R and N S each equal to
E. With centre O, radius O R, describe an arc. With centre
Q of the given circle and radius Q S describe another to
intersect in T or V. This is the centre of the other circle.

Problems 100 and 101.—*To describe a circle to touch two given
circles L and M, one of them in a given point K.*

Join L, the centre, with K, and produce. Make K N equal to
the radius of the circle M. Join N and M and bisect it by a
perpendicular. The intersection O with L K produced is the
centre, and O K is the radius.

Note.—In working problems of this kind, of which there is a great
variety, the student should bear in mind the principles which are enunciated
at the head of Lessons XI., XII., XIII., and XV. In a case of doubt or
difficulty, he will find much valuable assistance by first adopting the analytic
method. Thus:—Make a sketch of the required figure, supposing it to be
completed. Then endeavour to find out, by working backwards, as it were,
what principles can be best employed to bring about this result.

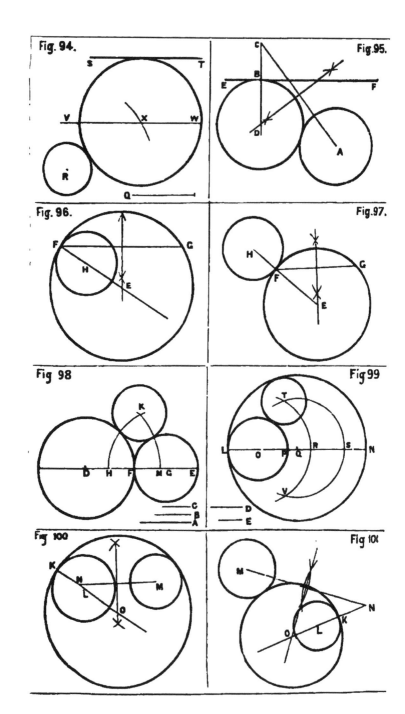

Fig. 94.

S
T
V
X
W
R
Q

Fig. 95.

C
B
E
F
D
A

Fig. 96.

F
G
H
E

Fig. 97.

H
G
F
E

Fig 98

K
D
H
F
M
G
E
C
B
A

Fig 99

T
L
O
P
Q
R
S
N
V
D
E

Fig 100

K
N
L
M
O

Fig 10(

M
N
K
O
L

Lesson XVII. — **RECTILINEAL FIGURES DESCRIBED ABOUT AND INSCRIBED IN OTHER RECTILINEAL FIGURES.**

"The sides about the equal angles of equiangular triangles are proportionals."—*Euclid* vi. 4.

"Similar rectilineal figures are those which have their several angles equal, each to each, and the sides about the equal angles proportionals."—*Euclid* vi. def. 1.

Problem 102.—*About a given triangle* A B C *to describe another similar to a given one* D E F.

On one of the sides, as A C, construct a triangle A G C similar to D E F (Prob. 14). Produce G C and G A. Through B draw R O parallel to A C to meet G C and G A produced.

Problem 103.—*About a given square* G H J K *to describe a triangle similar to a given one* L M N.

On K J construct the triangle K Z J similar to L M N. Produce Z K and Z J to meet the base G H produced.

Problem 104.—*Within a given triangle* O P Q *to inscribe a triangle similar to a given one* R S T.

On O P construct the triangle O A P similar to R S T. Join A Q. Through B draw B C and B D parallel to A P and A O respectively. Join C D.

Problem 105.—*Within a given square to inscribe an equilateral triangle.*

Draw diagonal E G. On E G construct the equilateral triangle E J G. Through H draw H K and H L parallel to J G and J E respectively. Join K and L.

Problem 106.—*Within a given triangle* A B C *to inscribe a square.*

From C draw C D perpendicular to A B. Draw C E parallel to A B. Make it equal to C D. Join E and A. Through the intersection F draw F G parallel to A B, and draw F H and G K parallel to C D.

Problem 107.—*Within a given trapezion* J K L M *to inscribe a square.*

Draw the diagonals M K and J L. Draw M N parallel to J L and equal to M K. Join N and J. Through the intersection O draw O P parallel to J L, and draw O R and P Q parallel to M K. Join Q and R.

Problem 108.—*Within a regular pentagon* S T O V W *to inscribe a square.*

Join O and W. Draw O X at right angles to O W and equal to it. Join X and V. From the intersection Y draw Y Z parallel to X O. Draw Y A and Z B parallel to O W. Join B and A.

Problem 109.—*Within a given sector* C D E *to inscribe a square.*

Join C and D. Draw D F perpendicular to C D and equal to it. Join F and E. From the intersection G draw G H parallel to D F. Draw G J and H K parallel to C D. Join K and J.

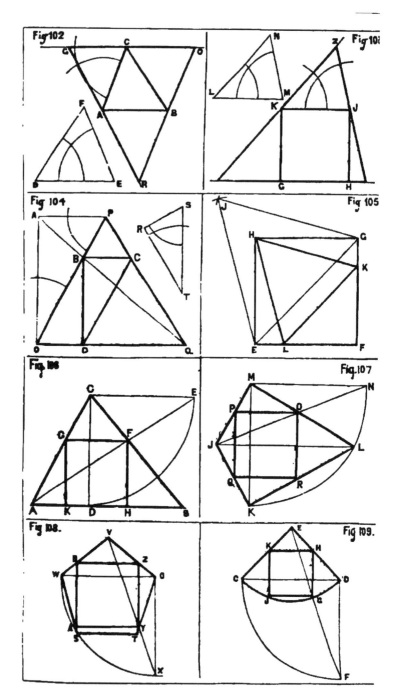

Fig 102

G
C
O
F
A
B
D
E
R

Fig 10

N
Z
L
M
K
J
G
H

Fig 104

A
P
S
R
B
C
T
O
D
Q

Fig 105

J
H
G
K
E
L
F

Fig 106

C
E
G
F
A
K
D
H
B

Fig.107

M
N
P
O
J
L
Q
R
K

Fig 108.

V
B
Z
W
O
A
Y
S
T
X

Fig 109.

E
K
H
C
D
J
F

LESSON XVIII.—**RECTILINEAL FIGURES INSCRIBED IN AND DESCRIBED ABOUT OTHERS**—*Continued.*

The diagonals of a square, as also those of a rhombus, bisect each other perpendicularly.

Problem 110.—*Within a square* W X Y Z *to inscribe another, one corner to touch a side at a given point* A.

Draw diagonals W Y and X Z. With centre E and radius E A describe a circle. Join the alternate intersections A, B, C, and D.

Problem 111.—*Within a square* E F G H *to inscribe another whose diagonal* J K *is given.*

Bisect the line J K in R. Draw diagonals. With centre M and radius R K describe a circle. Join the alternate points L, N, O, and P.

Problem 112.—*Within a parallelogram* B C D E *to inscribe a rhombus.*

Draw diagonals C E and B D. Assume any point A in one of the sides. Draw A M and produce to F. Through M draw G H perpendicular to A F. Join A, H, F, and G.

Problem 113.—*Within a rhombus* K L M N *to inscribe a square.*

Draw diagonals K M and L N. Bisect each of the four right angles so formed. Join the intersections O, P, Q, and R.

Problem 114.—*Within a regular hexagon* S T U V W X *to inscribe a square.*

Draw one diagonal X U and a diameter Y Z perpendicular to it. Bisect each of the four right angles so formed and proceed as in Problem 113.

Problem 115.—*Within an equilateral triangle* A B C *to inscribe a regular hexagon.*

Bisect each of the angles. With centre E and radius E A cut the lines which bisect the angles in F, G, and H. Join F G, G H, and H F.

Problem 116.—*Another form of the same problem.*

Bisect each of the angles. With centre O and radius O P cut the lines in Q, S, and V. Join P, Q, R, S, T, V, P.

Problem 117.—*About a given square* W X Y Z *to construct a regular octagon.*

Draw diagonals and diameters. With centre A and radius A W cut the diameters produced in B, C, D, E. Join the points B, X, C, &c.

Note.—The principle illustrated in the three last problems may be applied to any regular polygon. For instance, a regular octagon may thus be described in a square; a regular decagon in or about a regular pentagon, &c.

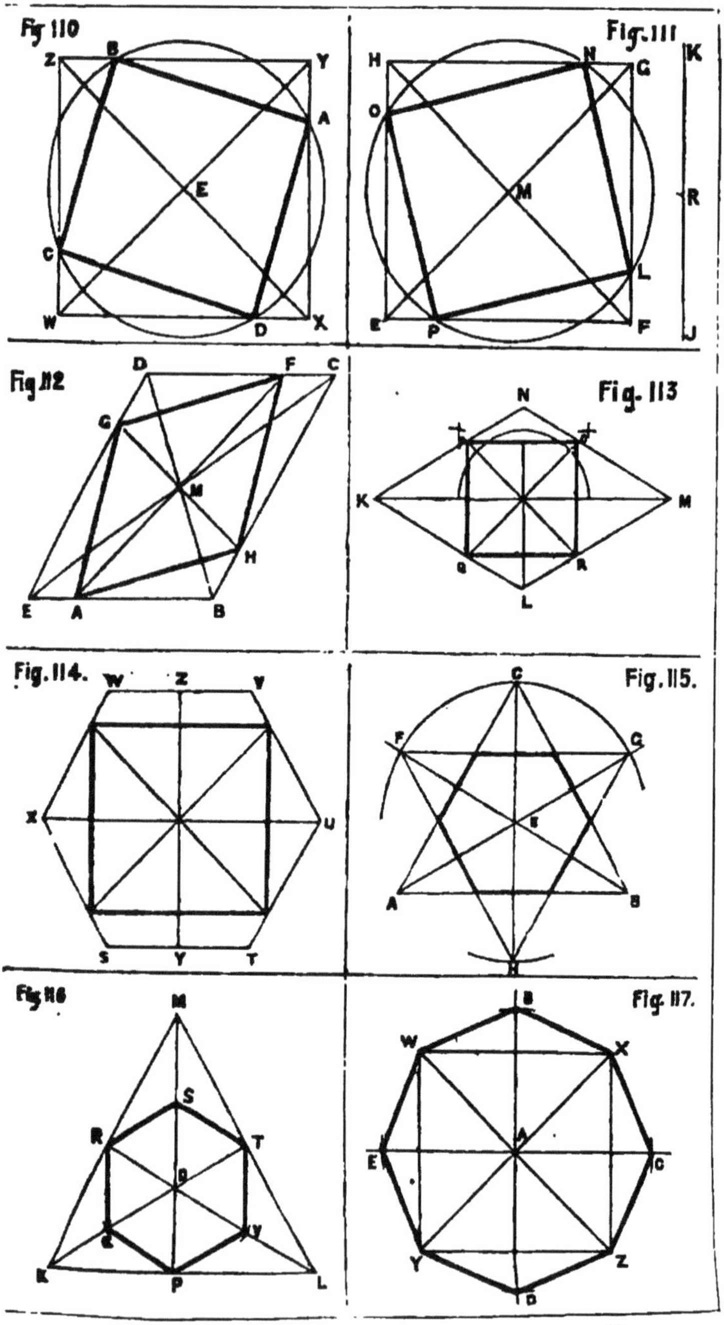
Fig 110
Z B Y A E C W D X
Fig. 111
H N G K O M R L E P F J
Fig. 112
D F C G M H E A B
Fig. 113
N K M Q R L
Fig. 114.
W Z V X U S Y T
Fig. 115.
C F G E A B
Fig. 116
M S R T O K P L
Fig. 117.
B W X A E C Y Z D

D

LESSON XIX.—RECTILINEAL FIGURES INSCRIBED IN
AND DESCRIBED ABOUT OTHERS.—*Continued.*

" The opposite sides (and angles) of a parallelogram are equal to one
another."—*Euclid* i. 34.

Problem 118.—*Within any quadrilateral figure* V W X Y *to
inscribe a parallelogram, given one side* A B.

Draw diagonals. From the extremity V of one of them mark
off V C equal to A B. Draw C D parallel to V W. Through
D draw D F parallel to V X; and D E parallel to W Y.
Through E draw E G·parallel to F D. Join G and F.

Problem 119.—*Within a triangle* A B C *to inscribe an oblong,
one side* D E *being given.*

With distance D E mark off A F. Draw F G parallel to A C,
then G H parallel to A B. Draw H J and G K perpendicular
to A B.

Problems 120, 121, and 122.—*Within a given trapezion, rhombus, or square* M N O P *to inscribe an oblong, one side* Q R *being
given.*

Draw diagonals M O and P N. From the extremity N of one
of them mark of N T equal to Q R. Through T draw T V
parallel to the side N O. Through V draw V W parallel to
M O. Draw V X and W Y parallel to P N. Join X and Y.

Problem 123.—*Within a given square* A B C D *to inscribe the
largest possible isosceles triangle, the base* E F *being given.*

Draw diagonals A C and B D. From A mark off A G equal to
the given base E F. Through G draw G H parallel to A B.
Through H draw H K parallel to A C. Join D with H
and K.

Problem 124.—*Within a given triangle* A B C *or any regular
polygon to inscribe another, whose sides shall be parallel and
equidistant from those of the former, one of them* D E *being given.*

Bisect the angles and obtain the centre F. Mark off A G equal
to D E. Draw G H parallel to A F. Through H draw H K
parallel to A B, and H J parallel to B C. Join J and K.

Problem 125.—*About a given triangle or any regular polygon*
L M N O P *to describe another whose sides shall be parallel and
equidistant from those of the former, one of them* Q R *being given.*

Find the centre as before, and produce the lines from the centre
through the angular points. Produce L M. Make L T equal
to Q R. Draw T V parallel to A L. Through V draw V W
parallel to L M. With centre A and radius A W mark off
X, Y, Z. Join the points and so complete the polygon.

Fig. 118

X
E
Y
C
D
G
V
F
W
A
B

Fig. 119

C
H
G
A
J
F
K
B
D
E

Fig. 120

P
W
V
M
T
O
Y
X
N
Q
R

Fig. 121

P
W
V
M
T
O
Y
X
Q
R
N

Fig. 122.

W
M
P
Y
T
V
N
X
O
Q
R

Fig. 123

D
C
G
H
A
K
B
E
F

Fig. 124.

C
J
F
K
H
A
G
B
D
E

Fig. 125.

Y
O
X
P
N
Z
A
L
M
T
W
V
Q
R

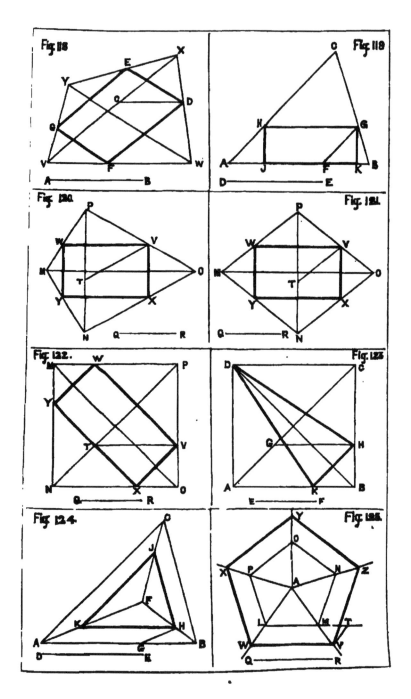

LESSON XX.—SEMICIRCLES INSCRIBED IN TRIANGLES AND SECTORS.

"The angle in a semicircle is a right angle."—*Euclid* iii. 31.

Problem 126.—*To inscribe a semicircle in an isosceles triangle* A B C.

Bisect the angle A C B by C D. Bisect the angle C D B by D E. Through E draw E F parallel to A B. Describe a semicircle upon F E.

Problem 127.—*In an equilateral triangle* G H I *to inscribe three equal semicircles, each to touch one side, and their diameters to be adjacent.*

Bisect each of the angles by the lines G L, H M, and I K. Bisect the angle I K H by K N. Through N draw N O parallel to G H, and N P parallel to H I. Join O and P. Describe a semicircle upon each of the lines O N, N P, and P O.

Problem 128.—*In a square* Q R S T *to inscribe four equal semicircles, each to touch one side and their diameters to be adjacent.*

Draw the diagonals; these divide the square into four equal triangles, in each of which a semicircle is to be inscribed. Draw the diameters, and proceed as in Problem 127.

Problem 129.—*Within any regular polygon (say a hexagon* U V W X Y Z) *to inscribe a number of semicircles, each to touch one side and their diameters to be adjacent.*

Divide the figure into equal triangles by drawing the diagonals, and inscribe a semicircle in each as before.

Problem 130.—*To inscribe a semicircle in a sector* A B C.

Bisect the angle A B C by B D. Draw D E at right angles to B D. Bisect the angle B D E by D F. Draw F G parallel to D E. Describe a semicircle upon F G.

Problem 131.—*In a given circle to inscribe any number of equal semicircles (say eight), each touching the circumference, and their diameters to be adjacent.*

Divide the circle into eight equal sectors (Prob. 45). Proceed as in previous problem. When the first semicircle K L M is found, take centre N and radius N M and mark off O P Q R S T. Join M O, O P, &c. On each of these describe a semicircle.

Note.—The inscribed figures in 127, 128, 129, and 131, are termed foiled figures of semicircular arcs when the chords of the arcs are removed; Fig. 127 in that case being a trefoil, Fig. 128 a quatrefoil of semicircular arcs.

Fig. 126.

C
F
E
K
A
D
B

Fig. 127

I
P
M
L
O
N
G
K
H

Fig. 128

T
S
Q
R

Fig. 129

Y
X
Z
W
U
V

Fig 130

B
G
F
A
C
D
E

Fig 131

R
Q
S
P
N
T
O
K
M
L

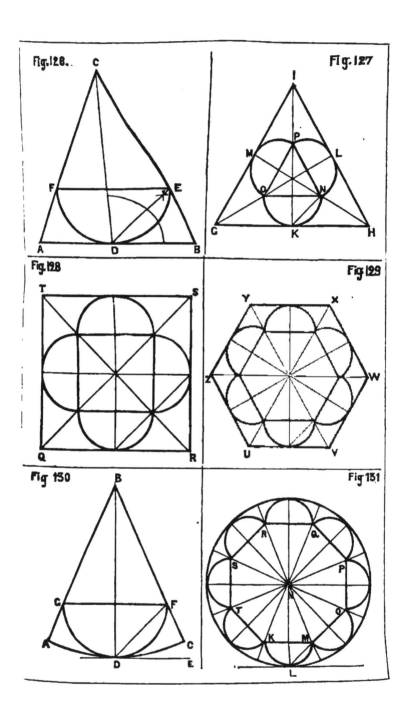

Lesson XXI.—SEMICIRCLES INSCRIBED IN QUADRILATERALS.

"The sides about the equal angles of equiangular triangles are proportionals."—*Euclid* vi. 4.

Problem 132.—*To inscribe a semicircle in a square* A B C D.
Draw diagonals A C and D B. Describe a semicircle on D B. Draw E F at right angles to A D. Join F and C. Through the intersection G draw G H parallel to F E. H is the centre, H G the radius. Construct the semicircle.

Problem 133.—*To inscribe a semicircle in a trapezion* I J K L.
Draw the diagonals. Describe a semicircle on J L. Draw N O perpendicular to L K. Join O and I. Through the intersection P draw P Q parallel to O N. Describe the semicircle with centre Q and radius Q P.

Problem 134.—*In a given square* R S T U *to inscribe four equal semicircles, each to touch two sides of the square and their diameters to be adjacent.*
Draw the diagonals and diameters. These last divide the square into four equal squares, in each of which a semicircle is to be inscribed. Proceed as in Problem 132.

Problem 135.—*Another method.*
Bisect the angle T R S. Through the intersection V with the diagonal U S draw W X parallel to R T. Describe a semicircle on W X. Through X draw X Y parallel to S U. Through Y draw Y Z parallel to R T. Join Z and W. Upon each of these lines describe a semicircle.

Note.—This is a shorter method than the first, and is based upon the principle of describing a circle to touch three given lines, viz., R S, S T, and T R. For if the circle with centre V and radius V W be completed, it will touch the line T R at the centre.

Problem 136.—*In a given equilateral triangle* A B C *to inscribe three equal semicircles, each to touch two sides of the triangle and their diameters to be adjacent.*
Bisect each of the angles by the lines A E, B F, and C D. Inscribe a semicircle in the trapezion C F G E (Prob. 133). Mark off G I equal to G H. Join H and I, P and I. Upon H I and upon P I describe a semicircle.

Problem 137.—*In any regular polygon (say a pentagon* K L M N O) *to inscribe a number of equal semicircles, each to touch two sides of the polygon and their diameters to be adjacent.*
Draw lines through the figure bisecting each of the angles, as in the last problem. Inscribe a semicircle in each of the trapezions thus formed.

Fig. 132.

D
C
G
H
F
E
A
B

Fig. 133

K
M
O
P
N
L
J
Q
I

Fig. 134.

U
T
R
S

Fig. 135.

U
T
Y
Z
X
V
W
R
S

Fig 136

C
F
E
H
P
G
A
I
D
B

Fig 137

N
O
M
K
L

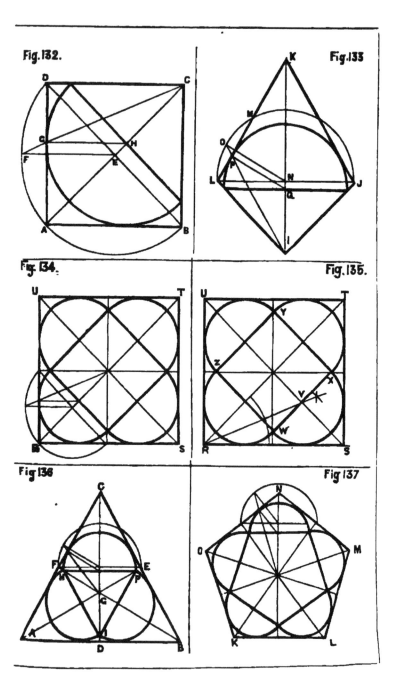

LESSON XXII.—**IRREGULAR FIGURES INSCRIBED IN AND DESCRIBED ABOUT THE CIRCLE.**

"The angles made by a tangent to a circle and a chord drawn from the point of contact are equal to the angles in the alternate segments of the circle."—*Euclid* iii. 32.

Problem 138.—*From a given circle to cut off a segment to contain an angle equal to a given one* C.

Draw a tangent E D to the circle at any point E. At E make the angle A E D equal to C. The segment A B E is the required one.

Problem 139.—*Upon a given chord* F G *to construct a segment of a circle to contain an angle equal to a given angle* H.

At one extremity F make an angle G F I equal to H. Draw F J perpendicular to F I. Bisect F G by a perpendicular to intersect in K. Then K is the centre and K F the radius. F J G is the segment.

Problem 140.—*Within a given circle to inscribe a triangle similar to a given one* L M N.

Through any point O draw a tangent P Q. At O make the angle P O R equal to angle L M N, and Q O S equal to M N L. Join S and R.

Problem 141.—*Within a given circle to inscribe a quadrilateral figure similar to a given one* T U V W.

Through any point X draw a tangent Z Y. At X make the angle Y X A equal to U T W, and Y X B equal to U W V, and Z X C equal to U W T. Draw C A and A B.

Note.— Only those quadrilateral figures can be inscribed in a circle which have their opposite angles together equal to two right angles.

Problem 142.—*About a given circle to construct a triangle similar to a given one* D E F.

Produce the base D E. Draw any radius G H. At G make the angle H G I equal to F E L, and H G J equal to F D K. Through H, I, and J draw tangents to meet each other. —*Euclid* iv. 3.

Problem 143.—*About a given circle to construct a quadrilateral figure similar to a given one.*

Produce the sides O P and M N. Draw any radius Q R. At Q make the angle R Q S equal to V O N, and R Q U equal to W P M, and U Q T equal to X M P. Through R S T U draw tangents to meet each other.

Note.—Only those quadrilateral figures can be described about a circle which have two opposite sides together equal to the other two opposite sides.

Fig. 138

C
A
B
D
E

Fig. 139

H
J
K
F
G
I

Fig. 140

N
L
M
P
R
O
S
Q

Fig. 141

V
U
W
T
B
Y
X
A
C
Z

Fig. 142

F
K
D
E
L
J
I
G
H

Fig. 143

X
M
N
W
P
O
V
T
U
Q
S
R

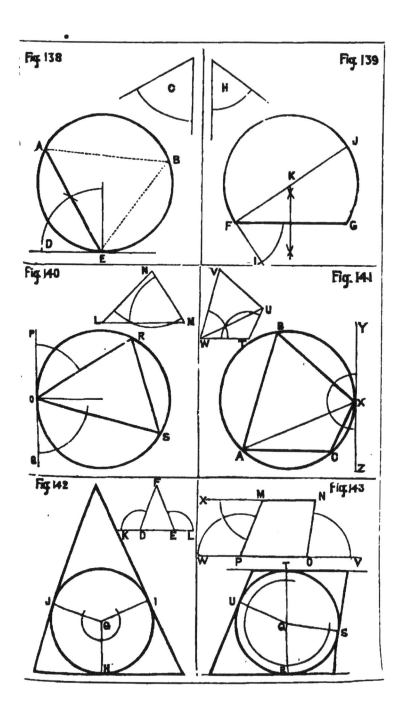

Lesson XXIII.—**THE CONSTRUCTION OF THE ELLIPSE.**

An ellipse is a plane figure bounded by one continuous curve described about two points (called the foci), so that the sum of the distances from every point in the curve to the two foci may be always the same. It is frequently, but erroneously, called an oval.

Problem 144.—*To describe an ellipse, its longest diameter (major axis)* A B *and its two foci* C *and* D *being given.*

Fasten two pins to a piece of thread or string, so that the length of thread between them may be equal to the major axis A B. Fix one of the pins at C, the other at D. With the point of a pencil draw the thread tight in the form of an angle. Move the pencil round from A to B, taking care to keep the thread all the while equally tense. In the same way describe the other half from B to A.

Note 1.—The sum of the distances that any point in the curve is from the two foci is equal to the major axis A B, i.e., the length of the thread. This is the principle upon which the construction of the two following problems is based.

Note 2.—The complete ellipse may be described without interruption as follows. Insert a third pin at one of the extremities of the major axis, or at any other point which may be given in the curve, and tie a thread tightly round the three; then take out the third pin, substitute the point of the pencil and proceed as above.

Problem 145.—*The major axis* E F *and the foci* G *and* H *of an ellipse being given, to find the minor axis (shortest diameter) and any number of points in the curve.*

Bisect E F in O. With radius O E or O F, half the major axis, and centres G and H describe arcs to intersect in U. Then U O U is the minor axis. Take any number of points in G O as P and Q. With E P as radius and G and H as centres describe arcs, and with radius P F (the remainder of the major axis) and the same centres G and H, describe arcs to cut them in J and N. With the same centres but with radii Q E and Q F the points K and M are found. The curve drawn through these points is the circumference of the ellipse.

Note.—If more points in the curve are required, an additional number of divisions must be made on the line G O.

Problem 146.—*To describe an ellipse, the major and minor axis* R S *and* T V *being given.*

Place them so as to bisect each other at right angles. As T is a point in the curve and R S is the length of the string: take T as centre and the half of R S, i.e., R W, as radius, and describe an arc to cut the major axis in X and Z. These points are the foci. Proceed as in the last problem.

Fig. 144.

A
C
D
B

Fig. 145

U
K
M
J
N
E
G
P
Q
O
H
F
J
N
K
M
U

Fig. 146.

T
X
W
Z
R
S
V

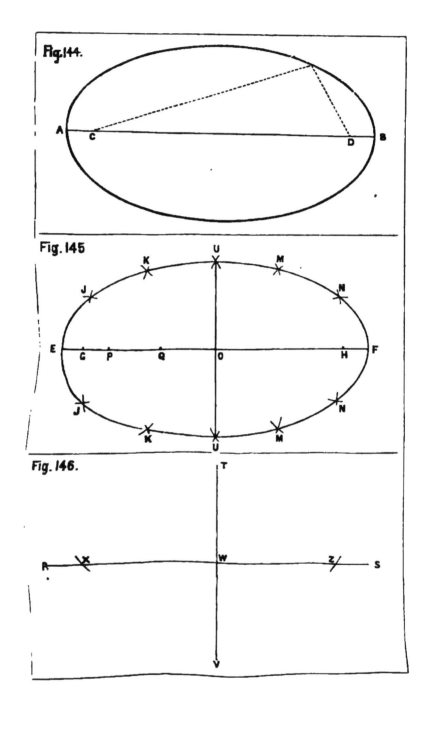

LESSON XXIV.—**THE ELLIPSE**—*Continued.*

Problem 147.—*To find the centre, axes, and foci of a given ellipse.*

> Draw any two straight lines H F and J K across the ellipse parallel to each other. Bisect them in points L and M. Join L and M, and produce the line to meet the circumference in N and O. Bisect N O in P. This is the *centre* of the ellipse.

> With centre P and any radius describe an arc to cut the circumference of the ellipse in three points, as Q, R, and S. Join Q with R and R with S. Through P draw T P U parallel to Q R, and V P W parallel to R S. These are the *axes*.

> To find the foci proceed as in the last problem. With distance T P or P U and centre V or W describe an arc to cut the major axis in X and Y.

Note.—By combining the principles taught in this and the preceding problem, we may complete an ellipse, given any portion of the curve greater than one-fourth. Draw any two parallel lines to intersect the curve and join their bisections as above. Should the line N O not terminate both ways in the given curve, then another pair of parallel lines must be drawn ; and the line which joins *their* bisections being produced, will intersect N O at the centre of the required ellipse. The axes and foci can then be obtained and the ellipse completed.

Problem 148.—*To draw a perpendicular to the curve of an ellipse at any point A, and a tangent at any point B.*

> Find the major axis and the foci (Prob. 147). From each of the foci draw lines through the given point A and produce them. Bisect the angle D A C. The line which bisects the angle is *a perpendicular* to the curve.

> From each of the foci draw lines through the given point B. Bisect the angle H B E. The line which bisects this angle is *a tangent* to the curve.

Note.—A tangent to an ellipse, like a tangent to a circle, is at right angles to a perpendicular to the curve, drawn through the same point.

An application of the first part of this problem to the construction of semi-elliptical arches is given on page 65.

Fig. 147.

V
F
Q
R
N
L
K
T
X
P
Y
U
H
M
O
S
J
W

Fig. 148

D
E
C
B
A
H
F

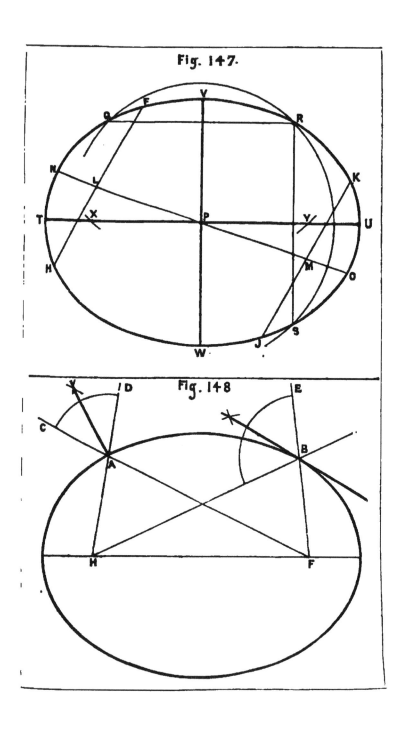

Lesson XXV.—THE ELLIPSE—*Continued.*

Problem 149.—*To describe an ellipse any two conjugate diameters,* P Q *and* R S, *and the angle made by them being given.**

Through R and S draw lines parallel to P Q. Through P and Q draw lines parallel to R S to meet the other two. Divide P T into any number of parts. Divide P U proportionally to P T (Prob. 34). From R draw lines to points 1, 2, and 3 on the line U P, and from S draw lines through 1, 2, and 3 on P T to intersect the others. Draw the curve from P through the intersection of 1 with 1, 2 with 2, 3 with 3, to R. Proceed with the remaining parts of the figure in the same way. The construction lines for one-fourth of the figure are here omitted in order to avoid confusion.

From the above problem it is easy to see how an ellipse may be described to pass through three given points which are not in a straight line, as A, B, and C. Fig. 149 *a*.

If we join any two of them, as A and C, bisect the line, draw from B through the bisection X, and make X D equal to X B, we have but to apply the above problem in order to complete the construction of the figure. In the same way an ellipse may be described about a triangle.

Problem 150.—*The major and minor axis* A B *and* C D *of an ellipse being given, to find a series of points in the curve by means of a straight-edge.*

Mark off on the straight-edge of a piece of stout paper or card-board the distance E F equal to H C (half the minor axis) and E G equal to H A (half the major axis). Place the straight-edge across the axis of the ellipse, so that point G may be in the minor axis C D and F in the major axis A B, and at the extremity E mark a point. This is one point in the curve, and any number of points can be so found by simply altering the position of the straight-edge, taking care, however, to keep G on the line C D and F on the line A B. The curve may then be drawn through these points.

The instrument called the Trammel, used by joiners and others for describing the ellipse, is constructed on this principle.

* A diameter is conjugate to another when it is parallel to the tangents drawn through the extremities of the other diameter.

The minor axis of an ellipse is a conjugate diameter to the major axis or transverse diameter.

Fig. 149

U
R
P
T
Q
W
S
1
2
3

Fig. 149.a.

B
A
X
C
D

Fig, 150.

D
A
H
B
O
E
F
G

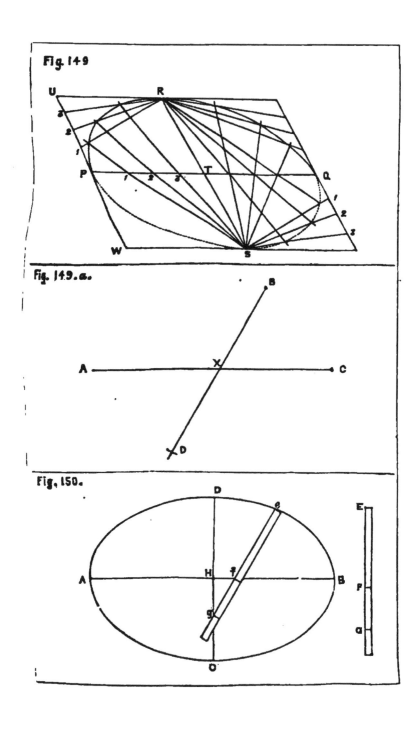

LESSON XXVI.—**APPLICATIONS OF PRACTICAL GEOMETRY TO PATTERN DRAWING.**

The student is advised to copy these drawings to at least twice the scale.

Fig. 151.—*A semicircular arch.* Divide the curve into the required number of equal parts, and then draw the straight lines forming the joints of the masonry. Notice that they all radiate from the centre.

Fig. 152.—*An equilateral (pointed) arch.* The centres from which the arcs are struck are at the springing of the arch. The faint construction lines show how the joints between the stones may be found.

Fig. 153.—*An obtuse pointed arch.* Here the centres are within the arcs. Two construction lines are drawn to show how the joints of the masonry are obtained.

Note.—The nearer the centres are to each other, the more obtuse the arch will be.

Fig. 154.—*An acute pointed or lancet arch.* In this case the centres are outside the arcs.

Note.—The further the centres are apart, the more acute the arch will be.

Fig. 155.—*A semi-elliptical arch.* First describe the ellipse, then divide it into the same number of parts as shown in the figure; and at each division erect a perpendicular to the curve, as shown in Problem 148.

Two sets of construction lines are drawn to remind the student of the method for obtaining these perpendiculars.

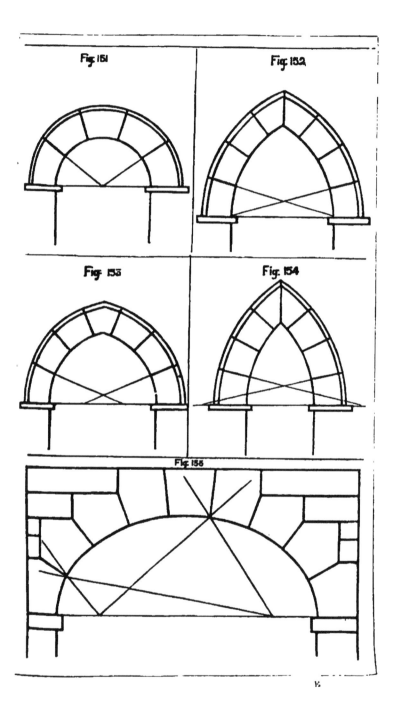

Fig. 151

Fig. 152

Fig. 153

Fig. 154

Fig. 155

LESSON XXVII.—**PATTERN DRAWING**—*Continued.*

The student should make enlarged copies of these examples, say to the scale of $\frac{3}{2}$ or $\frac{2}{1}$.

Fig. 156.—An application of Problem 115 to a simple and common arrangement of tiles or inlaid woodwork. The necessary construction lines are shown for one of the hexagons, from which the drawing of the rest can easily be made.

Fig. 157.—An application of Problem 116 to a simple design for a similar purpose. Here again the construction lines are given for one of the six repeated figures.

Fig. 158.—Another application of Problem 115. The skeleton of the figure, formed by the faint centre lines should be constructed first. The lines forming the boundary of the figure are then to be drawn parallel to the centre lines.

Fig. 159.—See note to Lesson XXVIII. Proceed with this figure as with the last.

Fig. 160.—Another application of the same principle. The construction lines will suffice to show how this figure is to be copied.

Fig. 161.—A third application of the same principle.

Fig. 162.—This example, it will readily be seen, is based upon Problem 117. The method of construction is shown in the first of the repeated figures.

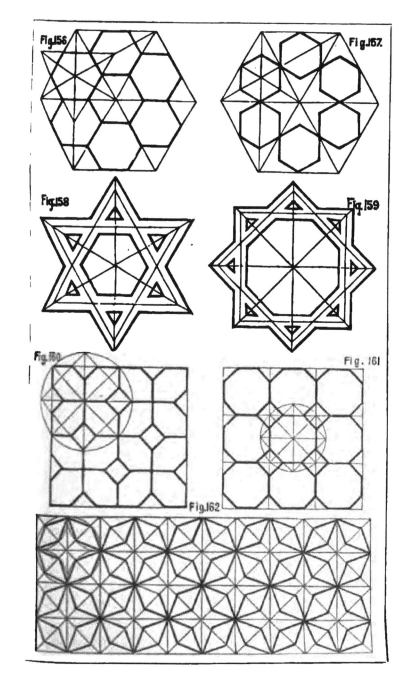

Fig.156 Fig.157. Fig.158 Fig.159 Fig.160 Fig.161 Fig.162

LESSON XXVIII.—**GEOMETRICAL TRACERY.**

The examples on the opposite page are a few of the many forms to be found in Gothic tracery for windows, doors, screens, panels, &c. For more elaborate examples, the student is referred to the various works on architecture, in the study of which he will see what an infinite variety of forms can be constructed on geometrical principles.

Figs. 163 and 164.—These are analytical diagrams of construction for Fig. 165. They furnish the student with the method of drawing the centre lines which form the foundation of the example—a trefoil within a circle, within a spherical triangle.

Fig. 166.—A quatrefoil of tangential arcs in a circle. This is but an elaborated form of Problem 91.

Fig. 167.—Another arrangement, based on the same Problem.

Fig. 168.—A trefoil of tangential arcs in an equilateral triangle. A reference to Problem 86 will suffice to show the student how to make a good copy of this figure.

Fig. 169.—A quatrefoil in a square, based upon Problem 82. Four circles in a square, with portions omitted.

Fig. 170.—A quatrefoil of semicircular arcs inscribed in a square. Problem 128 will enable the student to perform the necessary construction.

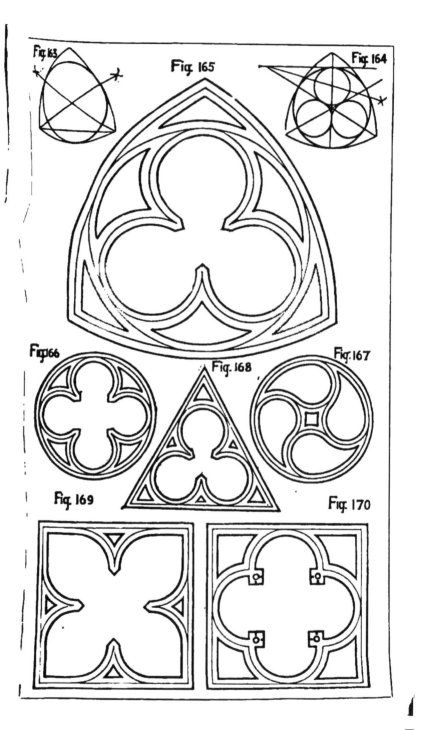

Fig. 163

Fig. 165

Fig. 164

Fig. 166

Fig. 168

Fig. 167

Fig. 169

Fig. 170

SOLID GEOMETRY.

Solid Geometry enables us to draw, on a flat surface, as that of a sheet of paper, which has only *two* dimensions, viz., length and breadth, the forms of solids which have *three* dimensions, viz., length, breadth, and thickness.

The following is a list of the simplest solid forms :—

A cube is a solid of six equal sides, each of which is a square.

A prism is a solid whose ends are parallel, equal, and similar plane figures, and whose sides are parallelograms.

A pyramid is a solid which has any plane figure for its base, and its sides triangles, which have a common vertex. There are various kinds of prisms and pyramids, as triangular prisms and pyramids, square prisms and pyramids, hexagonal prisms and pyramids, &c. They take their names from the shape of the base. A right prism or pyramid is one whose axis is perpendicular to the base.* If the axis is not perpendicular, the prism or pyramid is termed oblique.

A cylinder is that solid which is generated by the revolution of a rectangle round one of its sides. It may be defined as a round prism having equal and parallel circles for its ends.

A cone is that solid which is generated by the revolution of a right-angled triangle round the perpendicular. It may be defined as a round pyramid having a circular base.

A sphere, or globe, is a solid bounded by one convex surface, every part of which is equally distant from a point within, called the centre.

A tetrahedron is a regular pyramid having four equilateral triangular faces.

A hexahedron, or cube, has six square faces.

An octahedron has eight equilateral triangular faces.

A dodecahedron has twelve regular pentagonal faces.

An icosahedron has twenty equilateral triangular faces.

A segment of a solid is the part cut off by a plane parallel to the base.

A frustrum is that part of a solid next the base left by cutting off a segment. In a cone the part is sometimes called a *truncated cone.*

* The axis is a line passing through the middle of the solid from the centre of its base or ends. In a sphere any straight line passing through the centre and terminated by the surface may be the axis.

INTRODUCTORY LESSON.

Take some simple solid, such as a rectangular block of wood, or an ordinary brick, and place it flat upon a table or other horizontal surface. If we trace its form upon that surface, we shall have a drawing showing the *length* and *breadth* of the solid ; and if, whilst keeping it in the same position, we trace its form on the **wall** against which the table is placed, we shall have a drawing showing the *height* or *thickness*. The first is termed the *Plan*, the second the *Elevation*. Neither of these drawings alone is sufficient to determine the form of this solid ; we must have both before we can ascertain its actual shape and dimensions.

Though the drawings are on separate planes—the first on a *Horizontal Plane*, the second on a *Vertical Plane*, we can, however, represent them both on one and the same plane. Suppose we lay a sheet of paper on these two surfaces, to receive the traced drawings of the solid, as in Fig. 1.

It is obvious, that after having removed the solid and opened out the paper flat again, the desired result (Fig. 2) will be obtained.

The line X Y, represented by the crease or fold in the paper, is termed the *Intersecting Line*, for here the two planes intersect or cut each other. It will be noticed that the solid (Fig. 1), though it touches the table, does not touch the wall : its form can, neverless, be traced upon it by means of a pencil sufficiently long to reach from the solid to the wall, and held always in a position at right angles to that surface. We call the drawing, thus made, *a projection*, for each point of the solid is, as it were, cast or thrown on that part of the wall directly opposite ; thus *A'* is the projection of A, and *B'* of B.

These two drawings may, however, be obtained by a better method than that of tracing. Given merely the *dimensions* and *position* of this solid, its *plan* and *elevation* can be found. Suppose the dimensions to be 9″ by 4½″ by 3″ ; its position, lying flat on its broadest side, with its long edges parallel to the *vertical plane*.

If we construct a rectangle 9″ by 4½″ on the horizontal plane, with the long edge, 9″, parallel to X Y, which is common to both planes ; then project the extremities of these lines upwards, perpendicularly, to the intersecting line X Y ; produce them, measure off the height, 3″, from the line X Y, and complete the rectangle above, we shall have a more exact result than would be obtained by tracing.

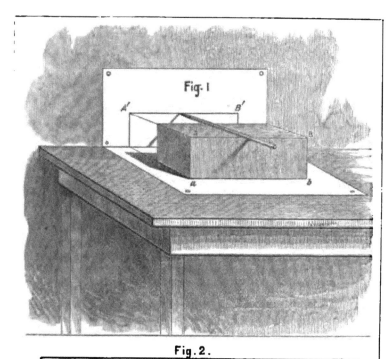

Fig. 1
A′
B′
a
b

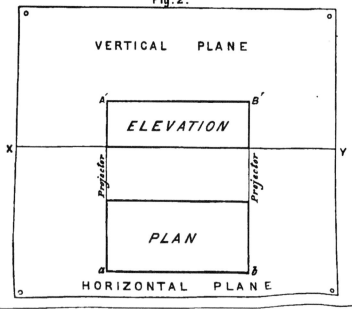

Fig. 2.

VERTICAL PLANE
A′
B′
ELEVATION
X
Y
Projector
Projector
PLAN
a
b
HORIZONTAL PLANE

SOLIDS IN SIMPLE POSITIONS.

Represent in plan and elevation the following figures :—

1. *A cube, standing on one of its faces, one edge of that face (3" long) to be parallel to the intersecting line.*

> First draw the intersecting line X Y. On the horizontal plane, *i.e.,* below X Y, construct a square 3" side.* Project the extremities of the sides up to the line X Y by perpendiculars. Produce these lines and complete the square on the vertical plane for the elevation.

2. *A square prism 4" high standing on its base, one edge of the base to be 3" long and parallel to the intersecting line.*

> Construct the square and project the extremities as before to X Y. Produce the perpendiculars, making them 4" long from X Y, and complete the rectangle above on the vertical plane.

3. *A square pyramid 4" high, standing on its base, one edge of the base to be 3" long and parallel to the intersecting line.*

> Construct the square as before and draw diagonals : the intersection is the plan of the vertex. Project the extremities and centre up to X Y. Produce the last perpendicular, making it 4" high from X Y, and complete the elevation.

4. *A cylinder 4" high, standing on its base, diameter 3".*

> Describe the circle, diameter 3", on the horizontal plane. Draw a diameter parallel to the line X Y and project up the extremities. Produce the perpendiculars, making them 4" long from X Y, and complete the rectangle.

> *Note.*—The elevations of the circular ends are straight lines.

5. *A cone 4" high, standing on its base, diameter 3".*

> Describe a circle as before. In this case the centre also must be projected. Produce it and measure off 4" on it and complete the elevation.

6. *A sphere 3" diameter.*

> Construct a circle 3" diameter, project the centre on to X Y and produce the line. Describe another circle, same radius, on the vertical plane, with its centre in that projector.

---

* The examples on the opposite page are drawn ⅓ the given size, to economise space. The student should, however, make his drawings the actual size.

Fig. 1

X

Fig. 2

Fig. 3

Y

Fig. 4

X

Fig. 5

Fig. 6

Y

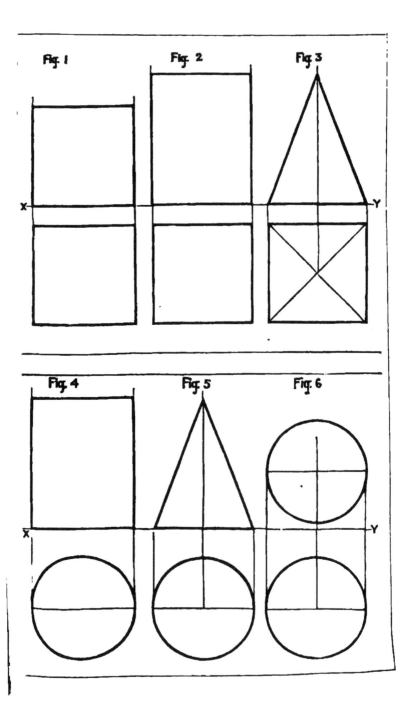

SOLIDS, WITH ONE OR MORE SIDES OBLIQUE TO THE VERTICAL PLANE.

7. *A hexagonal prism 4″ high, standing on its base, one side to be 1¼″ long and parallel to the intersecting line.*

On the horizontal plane construct a regular hexagon as required. Project the points *a, b, c, d* on to the line X Y. Produce these lines and measure off the height, 4″, on them, from X Y, and complete the elevation.

8. *An octagonal pyramid 4″ high, standing on its base, the diagonal of which is 3″ long and parallel to the vertical plane.*

Draw the diagonal *e f* as required, and construct the octagon. Draw the rest of the diagonals. Project the angular points and the centre on to X Y. Produce the latter line and obtain point *g′* 4″ from X Y. Join *g′* with each of the projected points of the base.

9. *An equilateral triangular prism 4″ high, standing on its base, one side of which (3″ long) makes an angle of 45° with X Y.*

On the horizontal plane draw a line making 45° with X Y. On any part of it construct an equilateral triangle (3″ side). Project the three angular points on to X Y, and produce above. Measure off the height 4″ and join the points.

Note.—The edge of the prism at the back is represented by a dotted line.

10. *A square pyramid 4″ high, standing on its base, one side (2″) makes an angle of 60° with X Y.*

On a line at 60° with X Y construct the required square base. Draw diagonals, and proceed as shown in the example.

11. *An equilateral triangular prism, 3″ long, side of triangle 2″, lying on one of its rectangular faces, the short edges of which make 60° with X Y.*

Construct a rectangle *c d e f* as required. Draw the line *a b* midway between and parallel to *c d* and *e f*. Project the angular points on to X Y. The height of the triangular ends will be equal to X *b*, which is the altitude of an equilateral triangle described on *d e*.

12. *A tetrahedron (a pyramid each face of which is an equilateral triangle), standing on one of its faces, with one edge (3″) of that face making 45° with X Y.*

Construct the base as required. Draw lines from the centre to each of the angles. Project each of these points on to X Y. The height is obtained by constructing a right-angled triangle, base equal to *p r*, hypotenuse equal to *r s*. The perpendicular *p t* is the height. Complete the elevation by joining the vertex with each of the projected corners of the base.

Fig 7

X
a'
b'
c'
d'
a
d
b
c

Fig 8

g'
e
f
g

Fig 9

Y
45°

Fig 10

X
60°

Fig 11

a'
b'
c'
f'
d'
e'
60°
f
a
c
e
b
d

Fig 12

p'
r'
q'
s'
Y
q
45°
p
s
r
t

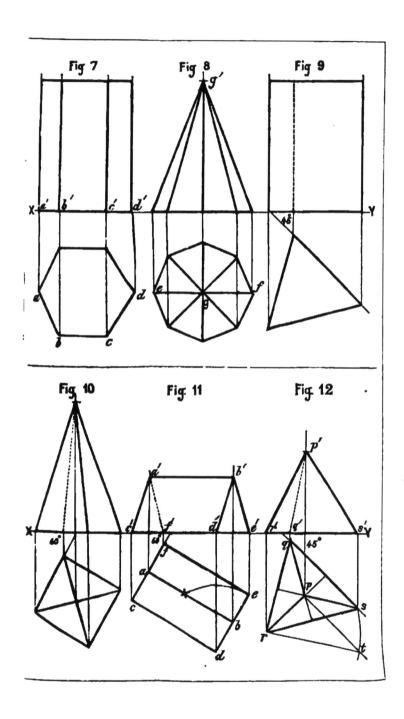

SOLIDS, WITH ONE OR MORE SIDES OBLIQUE TO THE HORIZONTAL PLANE.

13. *An equilateral triangular prism, 3″ long, one edge of triangular base (2″) at right angles to X Y, the base to be in a plane at 45° with the ground.* *

    Construct the equilateral triangle A B C ; one side B C at right angles to X Y. Project on to X Y. At *c′* draw *c′ a′* at 45° with X Y, and make it equal to *c′* D. Draw *a′ d′* and *c′ f′* perpendicular to *a′ c′*, making them each 3″ long. Join *d′* and *f′*. Project each of the points *a′, d′,* and *f′* on to X Y and produce them. Through A, B, and C draw lines parallel to X Y to intersect the projectors in *a, d, e,* and *f.* Complete the plan as shown in the example.

14. *A square pyramid (3″ high, one side of base 3″), lying on one of its triangular sides, the edge of the base on the ground to be at right angles to X Y.*

    First construct the plan and elevation, as if the pyramid stood on its base, with one edge at right angles to X Y. The elevation G H K must now be placed with the side G K on X Y. Project the points perpendicularly to X Y, to meet horizontals drawn through *k* and *g″,* and complete the plan.

· 15. *A cylinder (3″ long, diameter of circular ends 2″), its axis parallel to the vertical plane and at 45° with horizontal plane.*

    Draw the line *a b* at 45° with X Y. Draw *c d* and *e f* at right angles to it, making them each 1″ long on each side of *a b.* Join *c* and *f, d* and *e.* Project these points perpendicularly to X Y, and produce. For the plan of the axis draw the line *c′ e′* parallel to and anywhere below X Y. Then *a′* and *b′* are the centres of the circular ends, and *c′ d′* and *e′ f′* the plans of the diameters *c d* and *e f.* But the plans of the diameters at right angles to these will be equal to *c d* or *e f*; in other words, the width of the solid in the plan will be the same as the width in elevation. Mark off *a′* 1 and *a′* 2 each equal to half the diameter. The curve must pass through the points 1, *c′,* 2, *d′,* and will be elliptical. It may be drawn freehand or by means of paper trammel.

16. *A cone (axis 3″ long, diameter of base 3″), lying on its side, the axis being parallel to the vertical plane.*

    If the student has already studied Problems 14 and 15, a reference to the diagram, Fig. 16, will be sufficient to enable him to work this problem.

* *The ground* is a name frequently given to the horizontal plane.

Fig. 13

d'
a'
f'
X
D
C'
B
e
d
A
a
c
f

Fig. 14

K
h'
H
G
Y
k
h'
g'
k'
k''
g''
h''

Fig. 15

f
b
e
c
a
X
d
1
3
c'
a'
d'
f'
b'
e
2
4

Fig. 16

Y

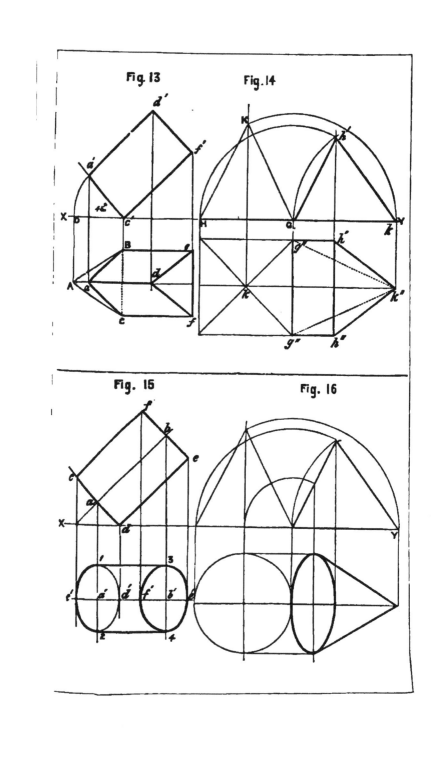

SECTIONS OF SOLIDS MADE BY HORIZONTAL AND VERTICAL PLANES.

Find the plan and elevation of the following figures :—

17. *A cone (4" high, diameter of base 3") in a vertical position. It is cut by a horizontal plane 1½" from the base.*

Construct the plan and elevation as shown in Problem 5. Draw the horizontal line *a b* 1½" from X Y.* Project point *a* down to cut the diameter of the circle in *a'*. With centre *c* and radius *c a'* describe a circle. This is the plan of the section ; and to distinguish it from the rest of the figure, parallel lines are to be drawn across it, as shown in the diagram.

18. *A sphere (diameter 3"), cut by a horizontal plane 1" from the centre.*

A reference to the diagram will be sufficient to enable the student to work out this problem.

19. *A hexagonal pyramid (4" high, side of base 1½") standing perpendicularly on its base and cut by a horizontal plane 1½" from the base.*

Commence with the plan, proceed to the elevation, draw *d e* 1¼" from X Y. Project down to cut the diagonals of the hexagon and complete the section.

20. *A square prism (4" high, side of base 2") standing perpendicularly on its base, one edge of which makes 30° with X Y. It is cut by a plane parallel to the vertical plane, ⅜" from the centre.*

Construct the plan ; draw *f g* parallel to X Y ⅜" from the centre of the square ;* project up the various points as shown, and complete the elevation.

21. *A cylinder (3" long, diameter of circular ends 2") with the axis parallel to both planes. It is cut by a plane, as in Problem 20.*

Construct the plan and elevation ; draw *m o* the plan of the section as required. With centre *r* and radius *r s* describe a circle or semicircle. The distance *m n* is half the width of the section in elevation. Mark it off from the centre *m'* and complete the section above.

22. *A hexagonal pyramid (4" high, side of base 1½"), axis in a vertical position. The solid is cut by a plane, as in Problems 20 and 21.*

Construct the plan and elevation, draw the plan of the section, *t v*, project up the various points as shown, and complete the elevation.

---

* For it has been shown that the elevation of a horizontal plane is a horizontal line, and the plan of any vertical plane a straight line.

Fig. 17.

a
b

Fig. 18.

Fig. 19.

d
f
e
Y

Fig. 20

30°
f
g

Fig. 21

S
r
o

Fig. 22

t
w
x
v

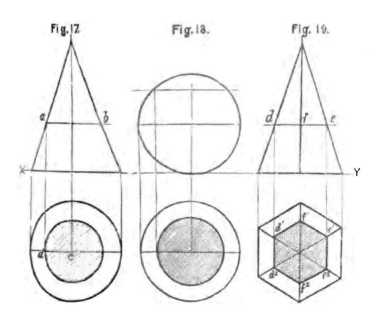

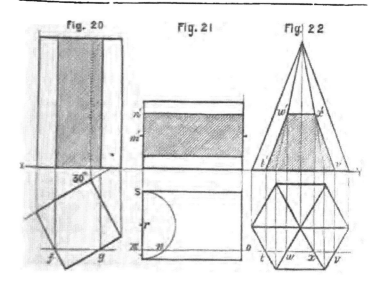

SECTIONS OF SOLIDS MADE BY OBLIQUE PLANES.

23. *A square prism (as in Fig.* 20) *is cut by a plane passing through the centre of the top and making* 60° *with the horizontal plane.*

Construct the plan and elevation. Draw $a\,b$, the elevation of the plane, making 60° with X Y. Project down point a; its plan will be the line $a^1\,a^2$. Complete the drawing of the section as shown.

24. *A hexagonal pyramid (as in Fig.* 19) *is cut by a plane at* 30° *with the ground, and intersecting the axis at* $1\frac{1}{2}''$ *from the base.*

Construct the plan and elevation of the complete solid. Draw $c\,d$ as required. Project down c and d; their plans are $c^1\,c^2$ and $d^1\,d^2$. Points e^3 and e^4 are yet to be found. Draw $m\,n$ at right angles to X Y, and project the plan on to it. Transfer the projected points on to X Y. Erect a perpendicular at s, 4″ high, and complete the second elevation (Fig. 24 a). Draw horizontal lines through c, d, and e, to cut the edges of the figure. The distance $e^1\,e^2$ is thus obtained. Transfer it to the plan as e^3, e^4, and complete the section there. Fig. 24 b is the true form of the section. The letters indicate whence the measurements have been obtained.

25. *A sphere, diameter* 3″, *cut by a plane,* a b, *at* 45° *with the ground.*

Project a and b on to the plan. The line $a'\,b'$ is one diameter, the other is equal to $a\,b$ in elevation. Draw the ellipse.

26. *A cylinder, as in Fig.* 21, *cut by a plane,* c d, *at* 30° *with the ground.*

Having constructed the plan and elevation, draw the axis. Project c and m on to the plan to cut the axis in c' and m'. Describe a semicircle on fg. Through d draw $d\,e$ parallel to X Y. From d' on the plan mark off this distance above and below in e^1 and e^2. Draw the ellipse through the points c, e^1, e^2, m^2, m^3.

27. *A cone, as in Fig.* 17, *cut by a plane,* n o, *at* 45° *with the ground, intersecting the axis* 2″ *from the base.*

Draw $n\,o$ as required and project points n and o on to the plan to intersect the diameter in n' and o'. This gives one diameter of the section. Bisect $n\,o$ in r. Through r draw $s\,t$ parallel to X Y. On $s\,t$ construct a semicircle; the distance $r\,m$ is half the other diameter of section. Mark it off from r^1 as m^2 and m^3, and complete the drawing.

Note.—The student is recommended to exercise the knowledge gained in Problem 24 by making second elevations of Figs. 23, 25, and 27.

Fig. 23.
Fig. 24
Fig. 24 a
Fig. 24 b
X
Y
a
b
a¹
a²
c
d
e
m
n
s
c¹
c²
c⁴
d¹
d²
e¹
e²
e³
e⁴

Fig. 25.
Fig. 26.
Fig. 27.
X
Y
a
b
b'
c
c'
d
d'
e
e¹
e²
f
g
m
m¹
m²
m³
n
n'
o
r
r¹
s
t

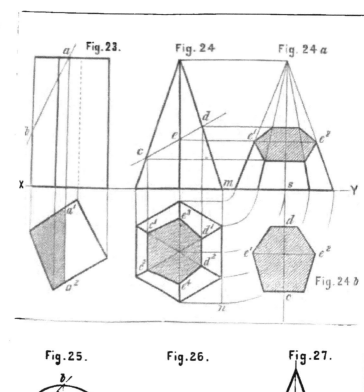

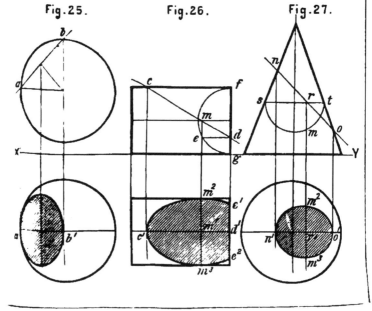

EXERCISES.

I.

1. Construct an equilateral triangle, side $3\frac{1}{2}''$.*
2. Construct an isosceles triangle, base $3''$, one side $4''$.
3. Construct a rhombus, diagonal $3\frac{1}{2}''$, one side $2\frac{1}{4}''$.
4. Construct a triangle, sides $3''$, $3\frac{1}{2}''$, and $4''$.
5. Construct a parallelogram, diagonal $3''$, two of its sides $2''$ and $2\frac{1}{2}''$.
6. Draw any irregular pentagon, and make another equal to it.

II.

1. Bisect each of the sides of an equilateral triangle (base $3''$), and join the points by straight lines.
2. Divide a line $3\frac{1}{2}''$ long into four equal parts.
3. Draw a line $3\frac{1}{2}''$ long, and erect a perpendicular to it $3''$ long at a point $2''$ from one end.
4. Construct a triangle, sides $3\frac{1}{2}''$, $3''$, and $2\frac{1}{2}''$, and drop a perpendicular from the apex to the base.
5. Draw any two lines to cross each other. Bisect each of the four angles.
6. Construct a triangle, sides $3''$, $4''$, and $5''$. Bisect each of the angles.

III.

1. Construct a triangle, sides A B, $3''$; B C, $3\frac{1}{2}''$; C A, $4''$.
2. Construct a triangle on a base $3\frac{1}{4}''$, similar to No. 1.
3. Construct an isosceles triangle, one of the equal sides $3\frac{1}{2}''$, one of the equal angles equal to A B C in No. 1.
4. Construct an isosceles triangle, base $2\frac{1}{2}''$, vertical angle equal to A C B (No. 1).
5. Construct a rhombus, one side $2''$, one angle equal to B A C (No. 1).
6. Construct a rhomboid, two adjacent sides $2\frac{1}{2}''$ and $3''$, contained angle equal to A B C (No. 1).

IV.

1. Construct a right-angled triangle, hypotenuse $3\frac{1}{2}''$, one side $1\frac{1}{2}''$.
2. Construct a right-angled triangle, hypotenuse $3\frac{1}{2}''$, and one angle half a right angle.
3. Construct a square, side $3''$.
4. Construct an oblong or rectangle, one side $3''$, the other $2''$.
5. Construct a square, diagonal $3\frac{1}{2}''$.
6. Construct an oblong, diagonal $3\frac{1}{2}''$, one side $2\frac{1}{2}''$.

* The sign $''$ represents inches. Feet are represented by $'$. Thus $2'\ 6''$ reads 2 feet 6 inches.

V.

1. Construct a triangle, sides A B, $3\frac{3}{4}''$; B C, $2\frac{1}{4}''$; A C, 3". Through the point C draw a parallel to the opposite side.

2. Draw a straight line X Y, $3\frac{1}{2}''$. Find a point W 3" from X and 2" from Y. From W draw a line making, with X Y, an angle equal to C A B (No. 1).

3. Bisect the angle made by two converging lines, without using the apex.

4. Construct an equilateral triangle, altitude 3".

5. Construct a triangle, base $2\frac{1}{2}''$, the angle at vertex equal to B A C (No. 1), and one at base equal to A C B.

6. Construct a triangle, perimeter 4", one angle equal to C A B, the other to C B A (No. 1).

VI.

1. Divide a line A B, $3\frac{1}{2}''$ long, into nine equal parts.
2. Divide a line C D, 3" long, into parts having the ratio of 3 : 4 : 5.
3. Find a fourth proportional, greater, to three lines A 2", B $2\frac{1}{2}''$, C 3".
4. Find a fourth proportional, less, to the same three lines.
5. Find a third proportional to two lines, A 2", B 3".
6. Find a mean proportional to two lines, A 1", and B $2\frac{1}{2}''$.

VII.

1. Construct a scale of $2\frac{1}{2}''$ to 1 yard, to show $5\frac{1}{2}$ feet.
2. A B (3" long) represents 2', 6"; produce it to show 3', 7".
3. Construct a diagonal scale to show $\frac{1}{100}$ of a line 3" long.
4. Construct a scale of 5" to 1 mile, to show furlongs and poles.

VIII.

1. In a circle of $1\frac{1}{2}''$ radius, inscribe a regular hexagon and an equilateral triangle.

2. In a circle of $1\frac{1}{2}''$ radius, inscribe a regular octagon and a square.

3. In a circle of $1\frac{1}{2}''$ radius, inscribe a regular heptagon.

4. Bisect a line 3" long by a perpendicular. Trisect each of the four right angles so formed.

5. Construct a scale of chords on a line 3" long.

6. Construct angles of 45°, 75°, 105°, with straight-edge and compasses alone.

IX.

1. Construct an irregular polygon, given the following :—
   Sides, A B $3\frac{1}{4}''$, B C $2\frac{3}{4}''$, C D $3\frac{1}{2}''$, D E $3\frac{3}{4}''$;
   Angles, A B C 110°, B C D 100°, C D E 105°.
2. Construct an irregular polygon, given the following :—
   Sides, A B 3.76", B C 3.26", C D 2.1", D E 2.24", A F 2.18";
   Diagonals, A C 5.36", A D 5.14", A E 4.52", B F 5.2".
3. Construct a figure equal to No. 1.
4. Construct, on a base of $2\frac{1}{2}''$, a figure similar to No. 2.

X.

1. Make a finished geometrical drawing of Fig. 56 to the scale of $\frac{3}{4}''$ to 1'.

2. Make an enlarged drawing of the above to $\frac{3}{2}$ the scale, or $1\frac{1}{2}$ times the size.

XI.

1. Describe a circle $1\frac{1}{2}''$ radius. Show how to find the centre.

2. Construct a triangle, sides $2''$, $2\frac{1}{2}''$, $2\frac{3}{4}''$. Describe a circle to pass through the three angular points.

3. Construct a regular polygon, having one side $1\frac{1}{2}''$, and one angle $135°$.

4. Construct a regular pentagon on a base $2''$.

5. Construct a regular hexagon, side $2''$.

6. Construct a regular octagon, diagonal $3\frac{1}{2}''$.

XII.

1. About a circle, $1''$ radius, describe an equilateral triangle.

2. Describe a circle, radius $1''$. From a point $3\frac{1}{4}''$ distant from the centre, draw two tangents to the circle.

3. The centres of two equal circles (radius $\frac{3}{4}''$) are to be $3''$ apart. Draw four common tangents to them.

4. Describe two circles (radii $\frac{3}{4}''$ and $1\frac{1}{4}''$), their centres to be $3''$ apart. Draw four common tangents to them.

XIII.

1. Describe a circle of $1''$ radius to touch two lines, making an angle of $60°$.

2. Draw two lines as above. Describe a circle to touch both lines, one of them in point A, $1\frac{1}{2}''$ from the angular point.

3. Inscribe a circle in a triangle; sides $3''$, $3\frac{1}{2}''$, $4''$.

4. Inscribe three circles in an equilateral triangle, side $3\frac{1}{2}''$, each to touch two others and one side of the triangle.

5. In a square, side $3''$, inscribe four equal circles, each to touch two others and one side of the square.

6. In a regular hexagon, side $1\frac{3}{4}''$, inscribe six equal circles, each to touch two others and one side of the hexagon.

XIV.

1. In a regular hexagon, side $1\frac{3}{4}''$, inscribe a circle.

2. In a rhombus, side $2''$, diagonal $3\frac{1}{2}''$, inscribe a circle.

3. In a trapezion, diagonal $3\frac{1}{2}''$, one side $2\frac{1}{2}''$, another side $2''$, inscribe a circle.

4. In an equilateral triangle, side $3\frac{1}{2}''$, inscribe three equal circles, each to touch two others and two sides of the triangle.

5. In a regular hexagon, side $1\frac{3}{4}''$, inscribe six equal circles, each to touch two others and two sides of the hexagon.

6. In a regular hexagon, diagonal $3\frac{1}{2}''$, inscribe three equal circles, each to touch two others and two sides of the hexagon.

XV.

1. Within a circle, 2″ radius, inscribe five equal circles, each to touch two others and the given one.

2. Within a circle, 2″ radius, inscribe a quatrefoil of tangential arcs.

3. About a circle, ¾″ radius, describe eight equal circles, each to touch two others and the given one.

4. Draw two lines, making an angle of 30°. Describe three circles to touch one another and the two lines.

XVI.

1. Draw a line A B, 2″. Find a point C, 2½″ from A, 1″ from B. Describe a circle, centre C, radius ½″. Describe another, radius 1″, to touch circle and line.

2. Draw a line A B 3″. Describe a circle, ½″ radius, to touch it ½″ from A. Describe another to touch circle and line, the line at a point 1¾″ from A.

3. Mark two points, A and B, 2″ apart, and a third, C, 1½″ from A and ¾″ from B. Describe a circle, centre B, radius B C. Describe another to touch it in C, and to pass through A.

4. Describe three circles to touch each other, radii 1″, ¾″, and ½″.

5. Within a circle, radius 1½″, inscribe two others, radii ½″ and ⅞″, to touch each other and given one.

6. The centres of two circles, radii ⅔″ and ½″, are 1½″ apart. Find a point K in the circumference of the large one, 2″ from the centre of the other. Describe a circle to pass through K, and to touch and enclose both circles.

XVII.

1. About a square, 1¾″ side, construct an equilateral triangle.

2. Within a triangle, sides 3′, 2½″, 2″, inscribe an isosceles triangle, vertical angle to be 90°.

3. Within a square, 2½″ side, inscribe an equilateral triangle.

4. Within a triangle, sides 3½″, 3″, 2½″, inscribe a square.

5. Within a trapezion, diagonal 3½″, two sides 2½″ and 2″, inscribe a square.

6. Within a regular pentagon, side 2″, inscribe a square.

XVIII.

1. Within a square, side 3″, inscribe another whose diagonal is 3½″.

2. Within a rhomboid, adjacent sides 2″ and 3″, contained angle 60°, inscribe a rhombus, one diagonal of which is 4″.

3. Within a rhombus, diagonals 3″ and 4″, inscribe a square.

4. Within a regular hexagon, side 1¾″, inscribe a square.

5. Within an equilateral triangle, side 3″, inscribe a regular hexagon.

6. About a square, side 2½″, describe a regular octagon.

XIX.

1. Within a quadrilateral A B C D (A B = 3½″, B D = 3″, A D = 2″, B C = 2½″, A C = 3½″) inscribe a parallelogram, one side 2½″.

2. Within a triangle, sides 3½″, 3″, 2½″, inscribe an oblong, one side 1″.

3. Within a rhombus, side 2″, one angle 60°, inscribe an oblong, one side 2″.

4. Within a square, side 3″, inscribe an isosceles triangle, base 1″.

5. Within a triangle, sides 3¾″, 3″, and 2¼″, inscribe a similar one, having its sides parallel to and equidistant from the former, one side 1½″.

6. About a regular heptagon, side 1¼″, describe another, side 1½″, to be parallel and equidistant from those of the former.

XX.

1. Within an equilateral triangle, side 4″, inscribe three equal semicircles, each touching one side, and their diameters to be adjacent.

2. Within a square, side 3″, inscribe four equal semicircles, each touching one side, and their diameters to be adjacent.

3. Within a regular pentagon, side 2½″, inscribe five equal semicircles, each touching one side, and their diameters to be adjacent.

4. Within a circle, radius 1¾″, inscribe a cinquefoil of semicircular arcs.

XXI.

1. Inscribe a semicircle in a square (side 3″).

2. In a square (side 3″) inscribe four equal semicircles, each touching two sides, and their diameters to be adjacent.

3. In an equilateral triangle (side 4″) inscribe three equal semicircles, each touching two sides, and their diameters to be adjacent.

4. In a regular hexagon (side 2″) inscribe three equal semicircles, each touching two sides, and their diameters to be adjacent.

XXII.

1. Construct a triangle perimeter 5″, sides in the ratio of 5 : 4 : 3.

2. Construct an isosceles triangle, base 3″, angle at apex 75°.

3. In a circle, 2″ radius, inscribe a triangle similar to No. 1.

4. About a circle, 1″ radius, describe a triangle similar to No. 2.

XXIII.

1. Construct an ellipse, major axis 5″, foci 4″ apart.

2. Construct an ellipse, major axis 5″, minor axis 3½″.

3. Construct a semi-ellipse in a rectangle 5½″ × 2″.

4. Describe an ellipse about a rhombus, diagonal 5½″, side 3¼″.

XXIV.

1. Construct an ellipse, major axis 5″, minor axis 3″. Mark four points in the curve between the ends of the axes, and through each of them draw a tangent.

2. Make a tracing of the curve of the ellipse, No. 1, and show how to find the centre, axes, and foci.

3. Construct a semi-ellipse, major axis 7″, minor axis 5″. Divide the curve into seven parts ; at each division erect a perpendicular 1″ long.

XXV.

1. Construct an ellipse, by means of paper trammel, major axis 5″, minor axis 3″.

2. Construct an ellipse, given two conjugate diameters, each 3″, intersecting each other at 60°.

3. Describe an ellipse about a triangle, sides 3″, 2¼″, 1¼″.

4. Inscribe a semi-ellipse in a parallelogram 4″ × 2″, one angle 60°.

INDEX

TO

PROBLEMS IN PLANE GEOMETRY.

——o——

LONDON : BURNS AND OATES.

Lightning Source UK Ltd.
Milton Keynes UK
UKHW020628031121
393313UK00006B/351

9 781375 522854